STAGEOLOGY

STAGEOLOGY
How to Stage to Sell

MEGAN MORRIS

TATE PUBLISHING
AND ENTERPRISES, LLC

The opinions expressed by the author are not necessarily those of Tate Publishing, LLC.

Published by Tate Publishing & Enterprises, LLC
127 E. Trade Center Terrace | Mustang, Oklahoma 73064 USA
1.888.361.9473 | www.tatepublishing.com

Tate Publishing is committed to excellence in the publishing industry. The company reflects the philosophy established by the founders, based on Psalm 68:11,
"The Lord gave the word and great was the company of those who published it."

Book design copyright © 2012 by Tate Publishing, LLC. All rights reserved.
Interior design by Sarah Kirchen

Published in the United States of America

ISBN: 978-1-61777-101-9
1. House & Home / General
2. Design / Interior Decorating
13.04.08

DEDICATION

To my very supportive and loving family, my three children, Grace, Will, and JK, who have grown up during the process of developing this special staging program. There have been times the children were with me on jobs, drawing quietly while I was setting tables and adding finishing touches. There were also times in our family Suburban when it was filled to the top with greens and trees and the children were peeking through the branches. We used to laugh about how it seemed like a jungle, and we would play "Going on a Lion Hunt" all the way home.

Also, special thanks to my parents, who are the most loving and selfless people I know. Without their love and support I would not have had the time to write down all of the methods that make staging so successful.

TABLE OF CONTENTS

FOREWORD

When I hear the name Walt Disney Company, it stirs up all kinds of thoughts in my head—magic, creativity, imagination, and whimsy. While the Walt Disney Company has a lot in common with other companies, the main difference is that Disney sells dreams and experiences, while most companies sell a product or service.

Megan Morris, the founder and visionary behind MHM Professional Staging, has incorporated form and function to create warm, inviting environments. This book details some of the efforts behind Megan's magic and how she creates *wow* impressions and lasting memories to everyone who walks into one of her professionally staged homes. Megan's skill set brings rooms to life, while dining and living areas become filled with ambience, thereby making a simple house a home. The features and benefits of staging have more than proven to be effective, and the response has been overwhelmingly favorable. Most realtors have found that we all share many of the same challenges when it comes to selling a home, and, to be sure, we all share the same common goal: to leave lasting impressions, a memorable experience, and well-satisfied consumers.

As the founder and visionary behind one of the largest real estate organizations, RE/MAX Town Centre, I have found the art of staging to be one of the most effective ways to market an empty home. Several years ago, we had a property that sat on the market for several months, despite an abundance of showings and presentations. Our sales professional engaged the services of Megan Morris to bring the home to life and create an inviting setting. Megan painted some accent walls, rearranged some furniture, brought in some additional pieces and accessories, and within a few days she created a setting that was stimulating but peaceful. We called back some of the customers who had previously viewed the home before staging, and the results were remarkable. The customers who viewed the home one week prior to staging returned only to see what they called "a home that was covered with pixie dust" in a setting that few could create. The couple looked at each other and simply said, "Sold."

I hope you find this book to be both interesting and useful and that it will give you some insight into the art of staging.

—*Charlie Orden, CSP, CDPE, CAM,*
Realtor, Broker, Owner
RE/MAX Town Centre, Orlando, Florida

INTRODUCTION

Are you trying to sell your home? Is it real estate ready? Have you taken every step to ensure your home can compete in today's market? If not, think again.

Consider the current mortgage environment. Even with the prime rate at historic lows, those for-sale signs up the street from you are yellow with age. In the nearly twenty years that housing price data has been collected, 2008 and 2009 have seen the biggest fall in home values. Just a few years ago, it seemed like everyone was getting home loans, whether they could afford to pay them back or not. And now, about-face: even people with good credit can't get loans. While housing values continue to drop, lenders have stopped lending. And due to soaring variable interest rates, many people are being forced out of their homes. Worse, the number of late mortgage payments continues to climb. In fact, U.S. foreclosures more than doubled from 2008 to 2009, and RealtyTrac believes 2010 foreclosures could top 2009 levels (2.8 million) and surpass the 3 million mark.

So, in times such as these, is your home *really* ready? What can you do to ensure your home will stand out from all the rest and attract a qualified buyer?

You can begin by thinking of your house as a commodity. You might not think about your home as a product, but when you get ready to place it on the market for sale, that's what it becomes. When there is a plentiful supply of houses on the market, you must think about how you can make your home stand out from the crowd and be a magnet for one of the limited few buyers out there to see your house as their next home—*and* at a price that is acceptable to you.

All products have features and benefits as well as pluses and minuses. The most successful suppliers go to great lengths to position a product successfully in the mind of their target audiences because they know that to effectively compete in the marketplace, products must be priced right, appeal to the needs of consumers, and look better than the competition. Homes are no different. As one of many for sale, your home must be presented to buyers in the best possible light.

When selling a house, everyone has the same goal—to sell quickly and at the highest price possible. The challenge is finding a way, beyond pricing and marketing, to compete in the market. One solution that is quickly gaining popularity is home staging. Home staging is a way of packaging a home to capture the attention of the widest variety of buyers.

Staging techniques focus on improving a property's appeal by transforming it into a welcoming, attractive product that the target buyer might want.

Staging is the process of preparing any home for sale, regardless of price, location, or market conditions. The official practice of staging increased in the 1990s, particularly on the U.S. west coast when the real estate market had hit a lull. Homeowners facing the frustrations of excessive inventory of unsold homes turned to new ways of selling. In more recent years, for many homeowners and real estate agents, the concept of professional home staging is proving to offer an advantage on promoting a home in the real estate marketplace.

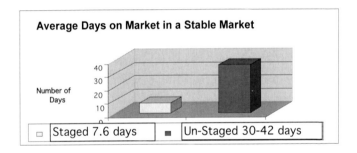

Today, home staging is a national trend that is raising the bar in the real estate market. In an up market, sellers stand to make more money when a home is staged, and in a down market, because there is an overwhelming amount of inventory and competition, staging can make a home stand out above the rest.

The goal of staging is straightforward: make more money in less time. There are countless examples of this being the case. Take a look at the chart above. According to a study done by Coldwell Banker in a stable environment, the averaged staged home is on the market twenty to thirty fewer days than a non-staged home.

From the same source, we can compare the average difference in selling price over list. In a stable market, for staged homes, the average selling price ranges from 3 percent to as high as 50 percent over list in some markets. Non-staged homes sell for an average of only 1.6 percent over list.

While the market, the economy, and industry are continually changing, many principles of preparing a home for sale remain constant. Regardless of the market you are in when reading this book, the principles within are timeless. The designs, plans, and trends of homes change according to the time, but the psychology of buying and selling a home remains the same. Most importantly, after fifteen years of experience in the real estate industry and being successful at both ends of the spectrum, I feel like I have seen everything and can offer inside information as well as exclusive insight into how to best position your home for sale.

Understanding the importance of staying current and observing and analyzing trends of buying and selling will help determine what's coming down the road. For instance, look into what kind of modifications are being made in new home construction and the reason behind those changes. More buyers are particularly keen to the growing interest in energy efficient and environmentally-friendly houses, and therefore an entire chapter has been dedicated to this important value.

Follow the simple yet proven staging tips and techniques in this book, and your home will stand out from the competition. Applied diligently, they may also reduce the sale time and increase the sale price of your home. You might choose to hire a professional home stager who will use a proven set of guidelines to evaluate and compare your home to present standards, and make any necessary adjustments. Or you might also do it yourself! This book is designed to help you do so. This quick-read guide will not only tell you *how* to stage, it will show you how to "read" the messages your home is sending to potential buyers and how to make the right choices in *staging to sell*!

WHAT IS STAGING?

Imagine you are the buyer driving up with anticipation to a house for sale with your realtor. You both enter the driveway, and immediately you see that the grass is overgrown, there are no flowers in the beds, and the house needs a paint job. The curb appeal is poor in your mind, and you have not even stepped foot in the house.

Your psyche is telling you the inside is probably not better than the outside, so you enter the house with a negative mind-set.

In contrast, let's start this scenario again, but this time as you drive into the property, the lawn is immaculately manicured with brightly colored flowers in the beds, and the house is freshly painted. The curb appeal is excellent, and you and your realtor comment on how well maintained the outside of the house is and enter anxiously anticipating a beautiful house inside. This is the remarkable difference to a potential buyer when viewing a staged home.

Staging entails the clever use of enticing elements to engage a buyer's mind, encouraging her to imagine how life can be in a home. The right packaging enables a buyer to visualize an ordinary three-bedroom, two-bath house as a home that she can and would want to live in. Staging, if done properly, works in any location or market conditions, regardless of price.

Contrary to popular belief, home staging goes well beyond decorating and cleaning. It's all about "dressing" your house for sale. Preparing your house for sale is akin to how you might prepare yourself for a job interview. In both instances, you research the prospect, polish your résumé, and determine how to speak to your best qualities. Then you decide how to "dress to impress." This is when you evaluate the small details, such as colors, accessories, and most importantly, how to look the part to "secure the offer."

Home staging is a key component of positioning a home for sale. Positioning is the process by which marketers create an image in the minds of their target market for a product. This process, if effective, facilitates a mental shift in the buyer's eye. According to Al Ries and Jack Trout in their book *Positioning*, this marketing concept is so simple that people often have trouble understanding how powerful it is. Positioning focuses on what to do to the mind of the buyer rather than what to do with the product.

Interestingly enough, what the buyer perceives often differs from reality. That's why industry experts sometimes refer to home staging as "selling a fantasy"—of the way people really want to live. Consider a Chanel television commercial that depicts a striking couple alone while music plays hypnotically in the background. Suddenly the message, "Share the fantasy, Chanel," appears. The commercial is saying, "Buy Chanel and this fantasy can be yours."

It is the same way you want to sell a home. An excerpt from an SFGate.com article, *Watching the Bluebirds Nest*, notes, "Staging is about projecting a lifestyle free from the mundane mess of our chaotic, high-tech, disposable culture and harking back to an era when there was time to fill one's house with fresh-cut flowers and stare out the window and watch the bluebirds nest." Staging is really about creating moods. When getting your home ready for sale, ask yourself what message you can send to take buyers to their "happy place."

Ideally, you should position your house in the mind of your buyer as a home that will fill specific needs or desires. Highlighting certain features will convey a message or feeling associated with "home."

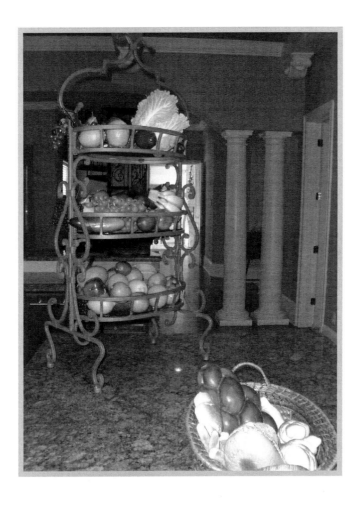

Here's an example. Imagine the person who just left your home and that night wrote in their journal the following:

After an exhausting day of looking at houses, all needing repairs I have no time for, the last home we went through finally felt like home. We were driving by when I noticed the for-sale sign and observed the mowed lawn, clean walkway, and beautiful flowers adorning the entrance. The front door looked freshly painted, and instantly something told me that I was in a special place. As we walked in, the house was warmly furnished with beige overstuffed couches and a chaise lounge with a book on it. The kitchen was immaculate and had a wooden bowl overflowing with fruit. There was also a familiar smell of freshly baked cookies in the kitchen, reminding me of my youth. As I wandered into the family room, I noticed a stone fireplace with logs already prepared and waiting to be lit. I imagined my childhood, reading by the fireplace and enjoying its warmth. There was also a faint sound of classical music in the home that made me feel at peace. The master bedroom was a sanctuary. It was so inviting with the quilt turned down on the bed and plump pillows waiting to be used. Of course I was looking for something much different, but this home seemed to have an aura of something special surrounding it, and I knew I had found my home.

You can see through the eyes of this buyer what it was that stuck out in their mind.

Selling a fantasy is delving into the little details. Clearly, the home described above invited this person to enter the fantasy of childhood or of a dreamlike place of comfort and warmth. This is a popular scenario: buyers looking for one house fall in love with one that did not originally meet their needs. How? By that mysterious appeal found in staging that makes the difference!

On more literal terms, staging is essentially creating a "stage" upon which a potential buyer can imagine her life being lived. In drama, the stage serves as a space for performers and a focal point for the audience. In the performing arts, staging is the process of designing or adapting the performance space for a play or film. This includes the visual detail and stagecraft elements such as costumes, props, lighting, scenic backgrounds, and sound effects that play a role in the dramatic unfolding. With these important symbols, the director crafts feeling that impact the audience. It is the same for the stager in selling a home: using props, lighting, and other visual tricks of the trade, she creates an emotion that appeals to the buyer.

WHY STAGE?
THE BENEFITS

Your house is probably your largest asset. Selling it can be one of the most important decisions in your life, so you want to ensure your house sells fast and for top dollar. Home staging is your best investment. Not only do you need your home to stand out amongst the competition, you want it to evoke an emotion so that potential buyers like what they see and feel compelled to buy it. Most home sales are a result of that overwhelming feeling of "I want it now." Your goal as a seller is to generate that feeling of "home" that will facilitate a quick and lucrative sale.

The greatest benefit of a staged home is that it will sell for more money in a hot market and sell faster in a down market. The real beauty of staging always works to a seller's advantage. If the housing market is sluggish, staging will give your home an attractive edge over the competition. If the market is strong and the home will likely sell regardless, you can use staging to increase the selling price.

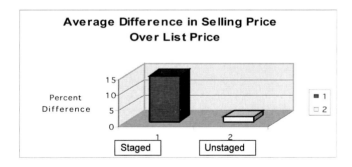

Let's take a deeper look at this. As in any market, your potential for selling your house will be governed by the laws of supply and demand. When demand is high and supply is constricted, it will be quite easy. However, when homes are in plentiful supply and demand is low, it becomes a real challenge.

Demand is influenced by many factors, but fundamentally, it comes down to the number of people who want to buy. And this in turn is influenced by whether mortgages are freely available, the interest rate that defines the cost of the mortgage, and whether buyers are confident about their future. On the other hand, supply is influenced by the number of homes for sale in a given geographic area and whether there is a healthy supply of new homes. When builders have unsold stock and banks are trying to sell homes that are the result of mortgage defaults, there is a plentiful supply.

When the market is slow-moving, the laws of supply and demand make the sale of homes very difficult. Buyers gain the upper hand. Supply becomes plentiful as a result of short sales and foreclosures. Demand then becomes constrained by the economic downturn, with rising levels of unemployment and constraints on mortgage availability. When this happens, home staging comes to the rescue. This unique system has proven to help sell homes faster and/or for more money in every market.

Another important reason to stage is because what people look for in a home is drastically different today than yesteryear. In years bygone, a home was simply a shelter. Maybe everything and everyone was in one room. But as time went on, more and more rooms were added to a home to serve specific functions. Individual bedrooms came on to the scene. In the 1960s, more than one bathroom became the standard. In the last decade, we've seen the emerging demand for home offices and theaters. And mudrooms have made a comeback.

Even the purpose of many rooms has evolved over the years. For example, some of us remember growing up when the entertaining was done in the formal living room. The kitchen was small and served mainly for the preparation of the food. But today, the kitchen is the heart of the home—it's used for entertaining, and the formal living room has almost become extinct. When you walk into a house that has this relic of a room, you find it now serving as an office, a recreation room, or maybe even closed off to save on electricity.

In essence, our homes are now an extension of how we live and of our personality. Because the way you live in your home is different than the way you sell it, staging becomes essential. And every home is different, so staging is a way of preparing it to stand out from the competition by making it impressive and memorable. "Whether it encompasses little more than adding fresh flowers and removing clutter, or involves hauling away and replacing major pieces of furniture, the goal of staging is putting a house's best foot forward and giving it the gloss of a marketable commodity," advises Barb Schwarz, a California-based real estate practitioner who first coined the word "staging" back in the 1970s. Schwarz goes on to say, "The home should be staged, whether it is an eighty-thousand dollar house or a four-million dollar one. Homes that are staged sell faster in slow markets and at higher prices in stronger markets."

Today's buyers are busy, usually a dual-income family, needing to quickly get on with their lives. Most buyers look for a house that is "move-in ready"—they aren't interested in moving into a home that requires "move-in repairs." If staged, real estate agents will have great confidence in showing your home to potential buyers because they know it is *ready* to be sold. In fact, when a house is staged, the realtor has the option to put a "staged home" sign under the for-sale sign. Some savvy buyers will even ask to see a "staged home" *first*, knowing it will show best and will save them time and effort.

Staged homes attract the widest audience of viewers, targeting the potential home buyer because they are more appealing and are quickly earning a reputation of "the best properties to see." Buyers generally do not buy for potential. They want "move-in" condition property.

Staged homes maximize the best features of a house and minimize its faults. What you are striving for is a "love at first sight" response. It is interesting how many people start house-hunting in a very logical state of mind but ultimately end up buying for emotional reasons. A chief reason to stage a home for sale is to arouse the powerful feeling: I belong here.

Notes

HOW TO STAGE

This chapter takes you through the how-tos and details of the six major steps of staging. As a homeowner, you can stage your own house by following the steps outlined; however, if you do not have the time, bringing in a professional, accredited staging professional might be helpful.

Using Stagers

In past years, homeowners were left to their own discretion in preparing for home showings. More recently, real estate agents have begun providing valuable guidance on what factors can help sell a home, but even the more design-savvy ones might not have the time or level of expertise required to get a home into optimal selling condition without some experienced assistance. Stagers will come in and approach each room of a house as if each door frame is a camera lens. An article in the *Kiplinger's Personal Finance* real estate section points out that distinguishing your home from the competition can be accomplished by having your home staged: "Professional stagers can see your house as buyers will, and they'll set the scene so that buyers can imagine living there." Professional home stagers are practiced in the art of preparing a home for a most favorable resale. They are trained to see a seller's house through the buyer's eyes. They work with the "flow" of a home, eliminate clutter, recommend and arrange furniture, and even assist in enhancing curb appeal. With the assistance of a professional home stager, your house can make a notable first impression on potential homebuyers.

Bear in mind that stagers don't have to be interior designers. In fact, in some ways, staging is very *different* than design. While designers can personalize the home, stagers actually help take *away* the personality in order to appeal to the masses.

You find and select a professional home stager much like you would any other professional service—by asking around and getting referrals. Check with your real estate agent because many larger real estate companies offer access to a listing of professional home services in your area, and these services will have already been prescreened. When you contact a home stager, ask for an estimate. Most home staging businesses will provide a free estimate, so get several and compare. You will find that some charge by the hour and others provide a flat rate. And don't forget to factor in the condition of your home.

How Long Does Staging Take?

Staging can sometimes be accomplished by a one-hour consultation. Other times, a thorough staging job requires a several-week production. It really depends on the size and condition of the house and whether the house is occupied or vacant. Some homes just need a little polish and can be staged in a day or two, while other homes require extensive repairs. The results can be equally spectacular whether you dress your house in a day or in a month. If you bring in a professional stager to help you prepare the home for market, staging will be a carefully choreographed process.

You might be concerned about the time it could take to stage your home and wonder whether you need to move out and make sacrifices during the process. Rightly so, you might expect it will be difficult or impractical to live in a house that is positioned to sell. For your family's sake, perhaps you worry it won't feel natural to live in a staged house. These are understandable hesitations because as mentioned before, a house packaged to sell has a completely different feel than a house packaged for living.

Try imagining it as an adventure. Tell young children to pretend they are on a reality TV show or "playing house," and make it an exciting activity for the whole family! If you or your family is feeling some apprehension, remember the benefits of staging. Take comfort in the fact that according to research, a staged house will not be on the market long, so the conditions of living in a staged home should be short-lived.

The alternative presents a far worse situation. While it may feel more comfortable to live in a house with dog toys on the floor, dirty dishes in the sink, and an array of photo albums on every end table, that house has a much lower chance of selling quickly. When a buyer enters your home for sale, she wants to imagine her own personal items in your house and how it would feel to live in the house. Any reminder that the house is occupied by another person will turn off the buyer, and that thought of ownership may be overshadowed by the visual clutter of personal items belonging to the current owner all over the house. If you *want* to sell your house fast and for the most amount of money, then it is worth the minor inconvenience of living in a staged home.

Getting Started

It's time to get started. Examples, suggestions, tips, and illustrations are included on the next several pages that break down the art of staging in six simple steps. Follow the six steps and use the handy tips and checklists in the upcoming sections, and you'll be well on your way to a quick sale! Below is a quick look at the six steps.

1. See your home through the eyes of a buyer
2. Evaluate your opportunities
3. Create a positive first impression
4. Minimize, repair, and clean!
5. Redesign
6. Create ambiance

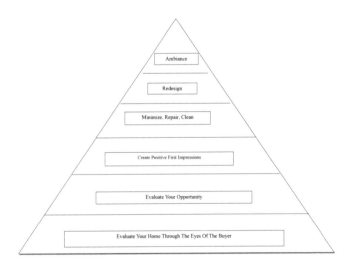

Step One:
See Your Home through
the Eyes of a Buyer

The very first thing you must do is envision your home as if you are the prospective buyer. Essentially, you have to detach yourself as the owner and occupant because it's difficult to look at your own home in the same way that potential buyers do. You become accustomed to the way things look and function, so you will overlook the faults. Therefore, you literally have to stop thinking of the property as a home and view it as a house—a commodity you want to sell for the highest dollar possible.

One of the best techniques for getting started and looking at your home objectively is to shoot a roll of film. As they say, a picture is worth a thousand words.

Begin by walking your property inside and out, pretending to be the buyer. Take a photograph of the first glimpse a buyer will have of your house. Next, stand across the street in front of your house and take several photos. Now, walk through the house, taking the route a buyer would follow, and snap a photograph of the first glimpse of each room and area. As you leave each room, take a picture to see where the buyer's eyes lead. Finally, walk around the entire home and snap pictures of everything a buyer will look at: the yard, pool area, garage, windows, you name it. Looking at your home through the eyes of the buyer gives you the first lead in the selling process.

Never leave it up the buyer to do the visual work. Create visual moments that buyers will respond to immediately as they view your house. For example, when a buyer walks up to the front door, she will be looking at the paint on the door, and she will notice if there are flowers in the surrounding area on the entryway. It will be critical to have a freshly painted or clean door; if there is a brass knocker on the door, you will need to make sure it is clean. You should have a nice plant or flowers at the side of the door.

The more pleasurable the impressions created, the longer buyers will want to stay in your house, and the more serious they will be to make an offer. Inviting elements engage a buyer's mind to imagine how life can be in this house. Creating not one or two but twenty-five to thirty-five powerful, indelible first impressions that position your house as a home is what enables you to sell both quickly and profitably. Other products that consumers purchase come carefully packaged, so a house, the most expensive product most will ever buy, should be no different.

Facilitating a critical mental shift in the buyer's mind is called positioning. Positioning is what the buyer perceives, not necessarily what it is. It is a marketing concept, described by Al Ries and Jack in their book *Positioning*, that is so simple people often have trouble understanding how powerful it is. Positioning starts with a product, in this case your house, but reflects what you do to the mind of the buyer as a home that will fit specific needs or desires. Simply highlighting certain features will convey a message or feeling associated with "home."

Step Two: Evaluate Your Opportunities

With your photographs spread out in sequence from first glimpse through the entire tour, evaluate the messages your house and its contents are sending. Carefully view each impression with buyer's eyes, anticipating how buyers will respond. Be critical: ask yourself, your realtor, or a trusted friend the old familiar question, "What is wrong with this picture?" What would a buyer see when she turns a corner? As she walks up or down stairs? Does each snapshot make a statement? If so, what is the message? Is it one of comfort? Tranquility? Stress? Disorder? These are the images you will be working with to create a first and favorable impression in every room. A room will produce stress in a buyer if it is cluttered, especially with personal items, if there is too much color in the room, and if the pieces of furniture are too big for the room. When you think of tranquility in terms of staging, it means a room will have order to it. Everything should be clean, and the room must be decluttered.

The goal of staging a home is to make it look and feel like the perfect place to bake cookies, relax, and take life at a slower pace, lulling in the serenity of old-fashioned family favorites. Work with your realtor to identify the potential needs and lifestyle characteristics of a possible buyer in your area and price range. For each room and area, think about what feeling you want to evoke or what message you want to send to "speak" to prospective buyers. Ponder emotions such as ease, abundance, newness, comfort, relaxation, organization, fun, spaciousness, nimbleness, luxury, and excitement.

Granted, some rooms are easier than others to evaluate for emotion. For example, a kitchen should feel functional and organized and suggest that meal preparation is easy and enjoyable. Closets should be neat and color-coordinated, rather than crowded and messy. Bedrooms should send a message of relaxation and refuge—maybe even romance. Above all, the feelings you want to convey are warm and systematic. You also want to ensure that your home doesn't feel personal to you so the potential buyer can see the house and its features, not your "stuff." The buyer needs to feel she is in *her* home, not in *your* home.

Step Three: Create a Positive First Impression

An important step in staging goes a bit beyond considering a buyer's perspective—it's vigilantly considering their *first* impressions. Again, never leave it up to the buyer to do the visual work. To give your home the competitive advantage, it is highly advisable to create impactful visual moments that buyers will respond to immediately upon arrival and continue creating that impact upon entering each room. Keep in mind that far less expensive consumer products come carefully packaged—wine, jewelry, cologne, even certain brands of shoes and lingerie. A house, the most expensive product most consumers will ever buy, should be no different. The more satisfying the impressions created, the longer buyers will want to stay in your house, and the more likely they will make an offer.

The buyer connects emotionally when she experiences a series of great impressions that best showcase the home and enable the buyer to visualize living there.

You can create powerful first impressions with simple things such as a freshly painted façade, colorful flowers in the yard, or a bouquet of flowers in the entryway.

The four most critical first-impression areas of a house include the following:

1. Curb appeal
2. The entryway
3. The kitchen
4. The bathrooms

Let's take a look at each one of these first impression components in more detail.

First Impressions: Curb Appeal

Curb appeal is just what it implies—what your home looks like literally from the curb. It is the view buyers see when they drive by or arrive for a showing. A large percentage of home buyers decide whether or not to look inside a house based on its curb appeal. That is why this is such an important aspect to evaluate in the overall staging process: you can't show a house if you can't get them out of the car!

Marketing and sales experts say that for the television medium, a sale is made or lost in the first three to four seconds. And studies also show that for print ads, 75 percent of the buying decisions are made at the headline alone. The same limitations apply in home shopping when prospective buyers are doing "drive-bys" with their agent or maybe on their own. According to recent research, most buyers form an attitude about a house within fifteen seconds! For this reason, curb appeal is the *first* area to address when evaluating a home for that all-important first impression.

Curb appeal is the first impression, which is a critical point to potential buyers wanting to go into a home. When evaluating curb appeal, borrow the rules of advertising. One evergreen rule talks about "selling the sizzle, not the steaks." It's the physical house that's on the market, yes, but the lifestyle it represents is sometimes more important. You want the potential buyer to see that your home provides more than just a place to live. Another advertising rule applies: "mystery of the seven veils." Translation:

you want your house to be intriguing and suggest there's more of where this came from on the inside.

If this is true, curb appeal stands as the most important of the four elements of creating first impressions. When staging, create something magical that lures the buyer inside.

We've already established that before homebuyers even step inside, they are judging the home's potential by its exterior. As a result, an unkempt or unattractive view of the outside of the home could turn a buyer away. Step back to the curb and take a good, candid look at your home. What do you see? What needs refreshing, repair, or rearranging? Then stand at your front door as if you are the buyer waiting for the door to be opened. What do you notice?

Landscaping

Landscaping is a very important aspect of curb appeal. In fact, in a *SmartMoney* article, it stated that landscaping could add up to 15 percent of a home's value. Walt McDonald, the president of the National Association of Realtors, advises, "When people ask me how they can get strong interest in their property, I always tell them to fix up their landscaping. If a homeowner is reluctant to do it, I tell them they won't get top dollar." After all, when buyers pull up to your home, it's not the luxury faucets or the gorgeous granite counter they see first. It's the landscaping. And if your lawn is patchy, your trees are on their deathbed, and your plants are a poor excuse for flora, it isn't going to matter what kind of magic you've worked indoors. Those buyers may keep on driving.

Immaculate landscaping pays off. You will not only attract more buyers and get a quicker sale; you will probably get a welcome boost in your sale price. "If you spend

55 percent of the value of your home on landscaping, and do it wisely, you might get 150 percent or more of your money back," says Massachusetts realtor Gill Woods. "And sometimes that number can go even higher. If your home's landscaping is on the low end for the area and you are putting it on par with your neighbors, you could be looking at a 15 percent rise."

The good news is you don't have to be a master gardener to work a few tricks of landscaping magic. Try little things such as placing potted plants at the front door and annuals along the walk or in clusters around a lamppost or tree. Line the patio or walkway with begonias and impatiens.

Color adds drama, but evenly lined greens and fresh mulch can also go a long way in creating a favorable impression. Do something fun like adding a birdbath! Also, a hanging flowering plant at eye level adds grace to a front entry, porch, or patio. If you have window boxes, plant fully with greens and flowers to create a flourishing, luxuriant look. If you don't have them, they are easy to install on brackets or a porch railing, and they give a dressed-up look to any house. (You can place them outside windows in condos and apartments too.) If it is winter, add pinecones. Curb appeal can mean the difference between a house sitting on the market for months or selling in a few weeks, maybe even days. Also in colder climates, an evergreen in a pot will make for a warm greeting. Or borrow a technique from Disney and try a few topiary pieces!

Look around your yard. Are there bare spots that could benefit from a few inexpensive plants or areas of the lawn that could use some sod? A weekend project might be well worth it! And while you're at it, make sure your mailbox is picture-perfect. Likened to advertising, this is your billboard! If it is an eyesore, replace it or paint it. Add new, bold numbers for better visibility. Although seemingly subtle, good maintenance makes a great first impression.

Lighting

Remember there's no rest for curb appeal—it's a 24/7 staging factor. Your home should be stunning day or night. If a buyer is serious about your house, they will drive by at different times of the day and night. Evening appeal is important, and lighting always helps with this. A popular strategy is to string low voltage lighting along your driveway, sidewalks, and around landscaping elements. (An extension cord and spotlight work well too, as long as it is put away during the day.) Add a decorative street lamp or an attractive light fixture to a front porch.

Solar versions of outdoor lights that are quick and easy to install are an option. If you have dimmers inside, try dimming the lights in the main areas of the house. Lighting that is visible through front windows enhances the home's appearance. Also, does the house appear safe? Lighting helps create a feeling of protection. If your house has an alarm, make certain the alarm sign is visible. Curb appeal should create an emotional desire to own the home and to live the lifestyle it represents. It's often the weed-out factor (no pun intended!) because many people might decide to drive right on past if the yard is barren or in ill condition. If you can get buyers through the front door, you have passed the first hurdle in selling it. The better your home looks at first glance, the more likely a buyer is going to see its potential—and the more likely to make an offer. Curb appeal can mean the difference between a house sitting on the market for months or selling in a few weeks, maybe even days.

There are some instances where overstaging in the curb appeal will turn off a buyer, and you need to be careful not to overdo your improvements. Too many planted flowers, planters, or statues in a garden are not recommended. This will create a cluttered look instead of an inviting curb appeal. When you are using planters, remember not to position them in the walkway or have planters that may overflow water or mulch to make the walkway unclean.

First Impressions: The Entryway

If you have lured the prospect out of her car and past your mailbox, congratulations! You are well on your way to staging success. She next arrives at your front door—the invitation to the dream. The front door is more than just an entry to your home; it is the beacon signaling a place of welcome. Make sure that the entryway—and landing and steps if you have them—is clean and free of cobwebs, dirt, and debris. The front door should be spotless and possibly freshly stained or painted.

If the front of the home receives direct sunlight, the door could be warped and cracked, and this must be addressed or the buyer is going to assume the house is not well maintained. Make sure door handles and fixtures are clean and possibly new if the old ones are too dated or barely working. The same applies if you have a kick plate, doorknocker, doorbell, and/or peephole. And regardless of your budget, spring for a new welcome mat!

The black ones with simple scroll designs are inviting and look nice with almost any house. For a final inviting touch, place pots of geraniums or other flowers near the front door.

In addition to the home's exterior, the foyer makes an immediate impression as soon as potential buyers walk through the front door. The foyer should be an inviting entrance that holds visual interest—not a drop-off spot for keys, jackets, or backpacks! In fact, your foyer *is* the "grand debut" of your staging experience: the curtains pulled back. Consider the foyer a prologue to the story your house has to tell, a compelling trailer for the feature attraction.

It is the first and last part of the house a buyer sees and as such leaves a first (and a last!) impression on whomever passes through.

A home's entryway can affect the mood of the home as well as its dwellers. According to Feng Shui specialists, the foyer sets the tone for the lives of those in the house. For example, the first thing one sees when entering a house can either positively or negatively impact the person passing through. In an article titled *Hello and Goodbye: It's all said in a Foyer,* by Sara Liss, she is quoted saying, "Space is also another consideration when designing a foyer. An open and spacious front entrance makes for greater flow and transition between the outside world and the home."

The foyer is the one space of the house where the entire essence of the house is established. I recommend if there is enough room to place a round table in the center of the foyer with a floral under a chandelier. But this can only is applicable if there is enough room in the foyer; the last thing you want to create is clutter in the foyer. The foyer is a place to greet guests, to check the mirror one last time before leaving, to enter grandly from a staircase above.

Is it warm and inviting? It should be if you want the buyer to continue their tour. Many people will walk right in a home and turn around and walk back out. Don't let this happen to you! Take the opportunity to grab their attention and invite them deeper into the home. On the next page is a first impression checklist that summarizes the key components of curb appeal and the exterior part of an entryway.

First Impressions: Bathrooms

First Impression Checklist
For Curb Appeal and Exterior Entryway

- ❑ Are you looking at the house as if you were the buyer?
- ❑ Is the curb appeal inviting?
- ❑ Is the doorway intriguing?
- ❑ Is the lifestyle projected positive?
- ❑ Is all maintenance kept up on sidewalk, mailbox, doorbell, front porch, and front door?
- ❑ Is there a loose floorboard or something that could creak or slip?
- ❑ Is the driveway free of cracks and mildew stains?
- ❑ Is the lighting updated, clean, and working properly?
- ❑ Did you check the home in all times of the day and night?
- ❑ Does the house look safe?Railings secured? Steps cleared?
- ❑ Is the front porch extremely clean—no cobwebs, wasp nests, dirt?
- ❑ Are the outdoor light fixtures clean, lightbulbs all working?
- ❑ Is the door perfect? Does it need to be painted? Hinges rust and squeak-free?
- ❑ Is the doorknob clean, polished, and new looking?
- ❑ If there is a knocker or kick plate, is it polished?
- ❑ Is there a welcome mat? And if so, is it clean and debris-free?

- Are shutters tight and freshly painted?
- Are all materials such as trash cans and garden supplies out of view?
- Is the lawn mowed and weeded? Planted areas in good shape? Mulch fresh? Leaves raked?
- Gutters clean and hanging straight? Drain spouts clear and rust-free?
- Roof clean with no missing tiles or shingles? Awnings free of debris and tears?
- Are windows clean and operable? Same with garage door?

In staging, *every* room makes a statement, yes, even the bathrooms. In fact, if a buyer feels uncomfortable in the bathroom, you may have difficulty selling to them. After all, you've heard people refer to the bathroom as the "throne" of the home! As a result, although you wouldn't think so, bathrooms are a key consideration in creating first impressions. For example, most bathrooms are never big enough. Make sure to maximize yours by making sure it is sparkling clean! Remember that cleanliness can overcome a size issue.

Bathrooms should be bright and cheery, not dark and dreary. Make sure your bathrooms have enough light.

If there is a window, have the blinds drawn to let in natural light. Of course, if it faces the next-door neighbor, you might want to make sure the landscaping outside is adequate. Updated fixtures are a nice touch, and using the recommended bulb strength will ensure success. You want it to be bright yet warm and welcoming.

Also, using small decorative items can spice up a bathroom. Try a plant, such as an orchid, or some kind of figurine if there is lack of space. If space is limited, rolled-up hand towels, pretty soap dishes, and a decorative picture frame can do the trick.

Before

After

Art on the walls is welcoming, particularly floral or scenic prints. Try to stay away from funny bathroom art that might offend someone.

Remember, you are trying to appeal to all the senses, so an air freshener adds a pleasant touch. Potpourri in a pretty bowl is also nice, or if you are going to be home, a fragrant candle is very welcoming. If the bathroom is really tight on space, using a scented fragrance and placing it on the floor out of sight can work too. Pretty towels, champagne in a bucket with two glasses, attractive soap dishes, florals, and candles are ideal for the master bathroom to create a romantic feel.

There are several things that should be avoided when staging a bathroom. Do not leave vitamins or personal items on the counters. No hand soap should be seen, only decorative soap. The counters need to be clean, and the towels need to match. You should remove all hanging robes and clothes, and the dirty laundry hamper should be placed in a closet.

You don't get a second chance to create a first impression! Below is a basic checklist to use when staging your bathrooms.

- ❏ Make sure bathrooms are squeaky clean and neat
- ❏ Paint   ❏ Color:
- ❏ Remove scum
- ❏ Clean grout and make stain-free
- ❏ Repair damaged countertops   ❏ Replace
- ❏ Repair flooring   ❏ Replace
- ❏ Repair sink(s)   ❏ Replace
- ❏ Repair leaky faucets   ❏ Replace
- ❏ Repair toilet   ❏ Replace
- ❏ Keep the toilet seat lid closed   ❏ Replace toilet seat
- ❏ Recaulk damaged caulk on shower, sinks, tub, or toilet
- ❏ Touch up/paint/refinish cabinetry   ❏ Replace
- ❏ Tighten or replace cabinet pulls
- ❏ Replace shower curtain   ❏ Add
- ❏ Replace window coverings   ❏ Remove
- ❏ Remove everything possible from counters and shower/tub area
- ❏ Hide the trash can
- ❏ Repair ceiling fan   ❏ Replace
- ❏ Bring as much fresh air into the bathroom(s) as possible

First Impressions: Kitchens

The kitchen is a strategic selling point for most buyers. In chapter two, we covered the dual function a kitchen serves in most homes today—cooking and socializing. For this reason, you want to create a favorable first impression of this central concourse. And you don't necessarily need to invest in a major remodel to make your kitchen appealing.

Homeowners spend more time in the kitchen throughout the day than ever before. Families gather to eat, cook, and clean up in the kitchen. It is without a doubt one of the most important rooms in the house. Because the fashion and materials of cabinets, countertops, and appliances are ever evolving, be aware that certain styles can really date the look and feel of your kitchen. If your budget allows, it is advisable to replace items that are over ten years old. If money doesn't allow, replacing the knobs on cabinets can help, and painting or staining cabinets can really freshen the look.

Something else to consider for your kitchen, if space provides, is an island. According to data collected by the National Association of Home Builders, the kitchen island is a "must have." An island can serve as a chopping board, a serving area, storage and food preparation, or even for dining. You can buy one on wheels that you can take with you. It is okay if the portable island differs in color from the cabinetry as long as it is clean and updated and seems to go with the style of the other pieces.

The lighting in a kitchen is very important, and changing a fixture is usually not very expensive and can be very impactful. The fixtures should be simple and not detract from the kitchen itself. As always, natural light is warm and welcoming; when showing the house, make sure the kitchen is as bright and light as possible. Also, make sure the walls look fresh, free from grease stains, and if papered, not peeling at the seams. If at all possible, consider painting the walls or adding a plaster texture. Or choose a wallpaper that has a subtle design to update the kitchen. Tone on tone in light colors works well. Fresh paint or paper is a lot less expensive and hassle-ridden than a complete remodeling but will still help to update the look of the most significant room in the house.

The most important staging aspect in the kitchen is to declutter and clean it. This can sometimes be difficult because most of us like to have the toaster, coffee maker, juicer, and all the other modern appliances within reach. However, keeping some of these conveniences undercover while staging provides the illusion of space. Use a basket for vitamins and other items you need daily so if a showing comes up, it's easy to place these things under the cabinets so counters look roomy and neat. There are several items that you can choose from to place on the kitchen counter, but they must be either new or in good condition and not look weathered. Things such as a topiary, a fruit bowl, a silver tray, and a new mat by the sink will add to the appeal of a kitchen.

You will have to double the effort in cleaning while your house is on the market. Keep every inch of your kitchen squeaky clean, including the tea towels! Remember, we're staging a fantasy that impresses the buyer with how easy life is in this home.

Following is a basic kitchen checklist to use when staging.

- ❑ Rearrange existing home furnishings and accessories
- ❑ Remove wallpaper/border
- ❑ Paint Walls   ❑ Color
- ❑ Appliances must be spotless
- ❑ If the appliances are included with the sale of your home, make sure they are operating and have proper documentation such as warranties and repair information
- ❑ Clean floors
- ❑ Repair flooring   ❑ Replace
- ❑ Replace or repair anything that sticks, squeaks, or drips
- ❑ Remove everything (notes, art, photos) from the exterior of the refrigerator door
- ❑ Pack everything that is now in your cabinets that is not used regularly. Cupboard space sells!
- ❑ Clear clutter from the countertops. Remove any appliance you don't use every day.
- ❑ Make sure sinks are clean and stain-free
- ❑ Repair damaged   ❑ Replace countertops
- ❑ Repair sink(s)   ❑ Replace
- ❑ Repair leaky faucets
- ❑ Clean tile grout and make stain-free
- ❑ Touch up kitchen cabinetry   ❑ Paint/   ❑ Replace Refresh
- ❑ Tighten or replace loose cabinet pulls
- ❑ Clean out pantry and organize all items to face front

Step Four: Minimize, Clean, and Repair!

Minimizing

When you sell your home, you know you are going to have to move. And when you move, you are going to have to pack. Most of the principles of staging require you to pack some of your things in advance of a sale. True, packing is work, but it's a necessary evil. A very important step in staging a home for resale is minimizing, so getting to it a bit early not only helps you get the inevitable task of packing underway, it helps you get top dollar for your home on the market. Minimizing includes both decluttering and depersonalizing, as well as what is referred to as "neutralizing."

Decluttering

Let's start with decluttering. Removing clutter calls for packing or hiding away those items that when left in view make a home looked lived in—personal items such as newspapers, books, collectables, crafts, works in progress, etc. Decluttering also involves organizing. The process of putting everything away neatly in its place in your house relays the message that it has a perfect spot for everything. Besides, decluttering makes every room in your house look and feel more spacious, freeing up space both literally and figuratively in your buyer's mind.

To effectively declutter, go through every room, every closet, every drawer, with this minimizing rule uppermost in your mind: When in doubt, throw it out. Or sell it or give it away! Pack away everything you can live without until after you move. The reality is that we can all live without much of the contents of our home. Do you really need the Lladro figurines out on display or the last two years' issues of *Better Home and Gardens*?

To declutter a drawer, take absolutely everything out of it. Some of the contents can be thrown or given away, such as makeup and old mail; the rest will be put in a basket and returned to their rightful places. What you'll discover is that staging has its side benefits—you will actually be simplifying your life! Before replacing the items, clean the drawer thoroughly. (There is no reason to come back to this drawer in the cleaning process!) Once minimized and clean, add drawer organizers to hold small items in place, removing any chance for the clutter to return after a few short weeks. Remember, organization gives the home a sense of order.

Like drawers, closets are apt to be cluttered. Potential buyers will want to inspect your closet space to see how much storage the house offers and to imagine *their* possessions neatly filling the space. If your closets are already packed tight, buyers will feel that there just won't be enough room for their items either. But if closets look organized, buyers will begin to feel their life could also be organized in this house. If you are selling your home in the winter months, pack away summer items, and vice versa. You'll be amazed at how much your closet space will grow!

In the process of decluttering, when returning items to the correct cabinet, shelf, or closet, use a common merchandising technique called facing. Facing is the act of displaying bottles, cans, and other items with the label facing outward. It generates a feeling of ease and organization and again makes your life easier! You'll be able to find the Band-Aids or the travel shampoos when you next need them.

The next time you go to the grocery store, notice how meticulously the shelves are faced. Take advantage of this concept to enhance the orderliness and appeal of your kitchen cupboards, medicine cabinets, bookshelves, closets and more. Face everything from toiletries and spices to books and board games. When facing games and puzzles, stack them with the largest box on the bottom and the fronts flush to create an orderly look. If bookshelves are packed full, remove half of the books, preferably the worn-out paperbacks, creating a feeling of spaciousness. Again, the first task at hand is to sort through and only keep what will be needed before the move. Cupboards are most attractive when they look well stocked, not crammed. Closets look the most appealing when there is space to add more, not when they are jammed to capacity. If you happen to be obsessive compulsive, your house probably already looks this way, but for the rest of us, when our homes are in a constant state of entropy, it is quite a task!

Perhaps the one room in the house that needs some real attention when it comes to decluttering is the home office. Due to the nature of this room's very function—where activities are usually works in progress—offices accumulate clutter. You want the office to send the message that indeed work gets done here yet downplay the emotion of stress that comes with any office-based task. A small portable water fountain and a well-positioned green plant can enhance the appeal of the home office—a space that might otherwise scream "work." Create a message of order and productivity by keeping desktops neat, supplies tucked away, and shelves orderly. Here are a few more tips on how to stage an office and still have it be functional for you.

- Rearrange existing home furnishings and accessories.

- Keep the desktop and all other surfaces as clear as possible. Move frequently used files to a vertical rack, or create one special drawer for quick access.

- Tuck any cords, cables, and wires out of sight.

- Eliminate any piles of paperwork from floor, credenza, desk, and shelves. Again, try assigning a special drawer or invest in a nice-looking in-basket.

- Straighten books, notebooks, and items on shelving and in closets.

- If at all possible, arrange the desk so that it faces the entry to the room.

- Keep overhead desk light on (even when it's daylight.)

- Keep window coverings open at all times, or even remove.

- Turn off computers and other equipment that cause a low buzzing sound or generate heat.

Next, let's discuss furniture. When a home is furnished prior to putting it on the market, there are usually more pieces of furniture than what is needed—or even desired—for staging. Many homes accumulate furniture over the years in response to families expanding or stylistic changes. Added pieces meant to be accents may actually crowd the room. Also, family members become attached to favorite chairs that stick around even when the intended replacements arrive on the scene. More often than not, when staging a home, it is necessary to remove several pieces of furniture so that each room looks fresh and open.

Remember, the primary goal is the sell the house, and therefore the only purpose furniture should serve is to complement the house—not the homeowner's taste!

In a dining room, scale and proportion are important to consider. If the ceiling tray is square in your dining room, then a round table should be used. And if the ceiling tray is rectangular, then an oval or rectangle table should be placed in the dining room. In the living room, only 50 percent of the space should be filled with furniture so there is an open, decluttered feel to the room. There are certain items that belong in a living room, such as a rug, sofa, or accent chairs, a coffee table, lamp, floral candles, books, fireplace screen, and piece of art or mirror to hang above fireplace with two candlesticks on either side.

Doors are another facet of staging that needs attention. While you might not generally think of doors as clutter, they can make an area feel much smaller and tighter. For example, doors that stand open most of the time—at the end of hallways or at entrances to kitchens, dining rooms, even basements—make a room feel smaller or block a great view. If you do not use a door, take it off its hinges and store it in the garage! The new owner can decide whether she wants to put it back. Remove closet doors that do not face the entrance of a room to give a more spacious look. This trick also works in areas that are tight or where a series of doors get jammed together.

Even the placement of houseplants needs to be evaluated in the staging process. Yes, houseplants are a great decorating tool because they add life and fill empty space as long as they are healthy.

But unhealthy ones—or too many—do just the opposite. If you are one of those people who like and have a lot of houseplants, thin the forest! Consider a few strategically arranged silk plants that don't need maintenance. Place them in decorative containers, baskets, or pottery that complements the décor. For open houses, nothing beats a bouquet of fragrant lilies in the foyer and blooming orange blossoms or jasmine around the entrance.

Depersonalizing

Beware the overtaking of a home by collectibles! Most homeowners aren't even aware of how great architectural and design elements, such as tray ceilings, pillars, and bay windows, can become lost with the arrangement of certain personal items. For example, showcasing a collection of porcelain teacups or decorative plates, lovely as they are, might upstage a beautifully carved mantel or shelf.

Prospective buyers either become engaged in the collection and lose sight of your home's natural features, or they become constricted by the claustrophobic feeling of too many things. For this reason, keep the family pictures, trophies, and collectables to a minimum. Carefully box them up and keep just a couple family photos in the bedroom or office. Remember, you want the buyers to see your house, not pictures of your adorable children. You want them to have the opportunity to imagine themselves in the house.

The importance of removing collectables and family heirlooms has already been addressed. Photos are another aspect of the home that usually needs neutralizing. Family photos are too personal to display when selling your house, as they sidetrack buyers from the business at hand. Many prospects get caught up in wondering, *Do I know these people?* Or they begin making unfounded judgments about the house based on the profile of the residents. (This is simply a safety measure too. Although the majority of people looking through your home are probably trustworthy, it is best to play it safe and not have too much on display.) For these reasons, remove and pack away personal photographs while your house is on the market. A photo here and there in an interesting frame on a bedside table or on an end table can, however, suggest a homey atmosphere. More than a few begins to come off as too personal.

Let's return to the topic of furniture. Sentimental pieces and family heirlooms may not only overcrowd the room or overtake the décor of a room, but if they're clearly cherished favorites, they might prevent the buyer from envisioning the home as her own. On the other end of the spectrum, there are instances on record in which multi-million-dollar home sales didn't go through because the new owners *wanted* the antique family heirloom chandelier. Avoid potential conflict by removing personal fixtures—the antique chandelier, the really cool propeller-like ceiling fan, the wall sconces your grandmother gave you, etc.—before putting your house on the market. If a potential buyer falls in love with a treasure that is moving with you, an argument and/or painful negotiation may ensue. Neutralize by replacing these fixtures with stand-ins before the house is shown. Otherwise, be prepared to part with them. Read on for more tips on neutralizing!

Neutralizing

Minimizing involves neutralizing. Neutralizing is taking the act of depersonalizing one step further. But it's an important step because it's impossible to anticipate the personal tastes and preferences of each and every buyer. A house that is presented in a way to appeal to one buyer might actually be a turnoff to another buyer who has completely different tastes. The best solution, therefore, is to neutralize the house as much as possible in order to appeal to the greatest number of buyers.

Any strong decorating element, whether or not it is attractive, distracts buyers. The unusual color or piece is what they will remember about the house. But a house with neutral paint colors, décor, and carpeting will accommodate anyone's decorating style. Neutral tones include earth tones, beiges, taupe, and buff. Painting is perhaps the most dramatic yet simplest neutralizing action. A fresh coat of light, neutral-color paint not only makes a room feel larger, it further enhances the feeling of clean, fresh, and new. Paint rooms that flow together—living room, dining room, kitchen, and hallways—the same neutral color to heighten the feeling of expansiveness. Paint offers the biggest bang for your staging buck. You also will want to remove or replace busy, dated, or bold wallpaper and carpets. Removing wallpaper with a rented steamer is easy, quick, and inexpensive; then paint the walls a light neutral color.

If the exterior of your house is already neutral, painting your front door a bright color can add some welcoming flair.

Also, if the house is beige and the trim is chipped and needs repainting, it would be best to use a color in a warmer hue like the house. Lighter beige, off-white, or the right shade of taupe work well. In addition, the two neutral colors—black and white—can be used in either the cooler or warmer tones.

The same goes for political or religious statements that are very personal. While important to you, certain messages might offend others or make them feel like they are intruding on your privacy if they disagree with the point of view. You do not want buyers focusing on your spiritual or political views. You want them to see and love your house. If a home is very much tailored to a specific individual, buyers can't envision it as their own. So keep the statues, signs, and other icons of beliefs out of view while staging.

Unfortunately but likely not surprisingly, pets need to be neutralized too. (*Note*: This is a different argument than neutering pets!) As much as we love our animals, any pets that live in your house can promote a strong, possibly negative statement too. Research shows that half of all potential buyers are either allergic to, dislike, or are afraid of pets. Not only might they shed and bring extra dirt into your home, all pets, no matter how well cared for, carry a distinct odor. If the buyers are allergic or afraid, they may not even come in. Do not fret if you have pets; you don't have to give them away! Just make sure you either take them with you when a potential buyer is coming over or have a cage in the garage. Sometimes neighbors or friends are willing to help out with dog-sitting during staging. Try scheduling the grooming or vet appointment at the time of a showing. Or take everyone for a car ride! In any case, make sure food bowls are out of sight and litter boxes are out of the house for the showing. You don't want your one hundred-pound—albeit friendly and clean—dog to greet your buyers, knocking them over in a friendly show of affection. (That is not a great first impression!)

Jokes aside with the above "neutering" comment, you do in fact want to make sure that your home is gender neutral when staging. For example, when walls, carpet, and bathroom tile are a traditional "girl pink" or "boy blue," seriously consider neutralizing with a coat of paint. (Or take those rooms to the extreme and go all out with gender-specific décor.)

Believe it or not, while sometimes subliminal, lines play a role when staging a home. For example, vertical lines are masculine and calming and give height. Combined with horizontal lines, things appear classical and strong. Curved lines offer personality, rhythm, and romance and tend to be more feminine. If lines or stripes are painted on walls, tone them down if they are bright, bold colors. If the stripes or lines are tone on tone, it should be fine.

On the other hand, if the lines are horizontal, like shelves, you can add items to give balance and downplay the rigid lines. For example, if there are many built-in shelves filled with many stacked books, instead of removing the shelves, especially if they were beautifully constructed, simply remove half the books. Add some greens or decorative pieces, such as boxes, to mix things up and to ensure your home looks more like a house than a library.

Also, if the home is predominantly decorated like a bachelor pad, consider using curvy sticks in an arrangement and add flowers. In contrast, if the home is more on the feminine side, bring in a contemporary sculpture, an arrangement with linear sticks, etc.

In summary, your house should offer as neutral an environment as possible so a buyer can find her dream house in yours. Again, most people are not particularly good at visualizing different furnishings or arrangements in a home, so they tend to think that what they see is what they get. The elimination of personal tastes, strong colors and posters, pictures, or other accessories that may distract makes it easier for buyers to imagine themselves there.

So what do you do with all this extra stuff? One option is, of course, to pack it and move it to storage, or to your next residence, if that's an option. As you declutter, depersonalize, and neutralize (and "de-pet!"), box up excess or outdated items for donation to a charitable organization in your area. Many charitable groups actively search for clothing, furniture, and other everyday items, and you will be helping others while helping yourself. Not only are you eligible for a tax deduction, you save the time involved in organizing a garage sale.

Decluttering costs absolutely nothing. In fact, if you sell the myriad of possessions you unearth while decluttering, you can actually make money. Finally, decluttering will make your upcoming move smoother. With everything in its place and no "extras" to ponder as you pack, the actual move will be quick and easy. Here is a summary list of minimizing tips.

- ❏ Pack up all family photos, diplomas, etc.
- ❏ Pack up all collectables, heirlooms, and special pieces that cannot risk being broken.
- ❏ Pack up clothing items you won't need in six months.
- ❏ Organize all closets, cupboards, drawers.
- ❏ "Face" all items so they look orderly.
- ❏ Clean up, trim, and take care of all healthy houseplants—remove all others.
- ❏ Check doors and other large pieces of furniture to see if necessary.

Cleaning

Now that you've removed the clutter and minimized the items in your house, let's get down to the basics: rolling up the sleeves and cleaning. And I mean cleaning like you've never cleaned before! People detail their cars—why not a house? When preparing a home for sale, it's time to get out the Q-Tips and clean every the little nook and cranny—around the sink, along the baseboards, under the burners, and so on. *Aren't you glad now you've minimized? Less to clean!* We're talking about an extreme clean. Get the carpets shampooed or steamed, the floors polished, the tile grout bleached, and hardwood refinished if it needs it.

When you are cleaning to stage, be sensitive to odors because buyers are! This advice isn't so much in reference to cleaning products but what odors prevail in your home that you might be accustomed to and not notice like a first-time visitor would. For example, excessive cooking or smoking odors, pet odors, and laundry and mildew odors will turn off buyers. If necessary, use room deodorizers or disinfectant sprays, or consider keeping windows cracked open for ventilation. As a last resort, cleaning with bleach will eliminate most odors. Heavy tapestries and draperies tend to hold in smoke, so this is a good time to clean or pack them.

When a buyer is going through your home, it's under severe scrutiny. The master bedroom might really spark her interest, and she begins to think seriously about your house. So she begins to look more carefully. Entering the master bath, she pulls back the shower curtain—and comes to a halt. A layer of soap scum covers the shower floor, and the grout is mildewed. Even though these two problems could be easily solved with a simple cleaning job, you've lost her. She can't see past the grime and begins to question the condition of the entire house. Even if she moves past that dirty bathroom, she will feel uncomfortable—tentative about opening other doors. And if she remembers your house *at all* later, it's a guarantee she will remember the shower floor. Dirty dishes in the sink cause the same reaction. Many buyers are very picky, and you do not want to give them any reason not to choose your house.

Perhaps the most difficult part of a house to clean and prepare for sale is the garage. But every buyer opens the garage door, takes a long glance at the size, a good whiff of the air, and a careful look at the storage space potential. If your home is marketed as a two-car garage, do your best to make sure two cars can indeed fit! This often means clearing out a lot of stuff. If you've got bicycles, sports gear, or gym equipment that is used regularly, you might have to make some temporary sacrifices or adjustments. Some of this equipment can be stored on racks and hooks or even go in the attic. Eliminate or store as much as possible to increase space. Make it possible for the buyer to imagine her vehicles and own outdoor and garden equipment fitting. Thankfully, there are several home improvement stores and services that offer containers and systems for garages that can be found in your local area by doing an online search. Consider having shelves installed or buy storage containers all of the same size so they look neat and orderly. Label each one to add to your organization. Here are a few garage cleaning tips.

- Remove any oil spots from floor.

- Clean and straighten tools and other equipment.

- Organize chemicals, parts, and toys into labeled bins.

- Clean out the refrigerator and freezer.

- Throw out or remove from view rusty tools or "unsafe" looking equipment.

- Remove cobwebs, wildlife traps, and bug carcasses!

- Eliminate odors with plug-ins, lava rocks, etc.

- Consider painting or using inexpensive outdoor wall-to-wall carpet if the floor is too old to repair.

- And don't forget the driveway, especially if it is in the front of your home! Give your driveway some real attention when cleaning—and when staging your first impressions. A driveway might not seem like much to you, but consider what it looks like to the arriving buyer. It needs to make a positive impression. Think of yourself as the buyer pulling up with the realtor and stepping onto the concrete. Worse case, if the driveway is muddy, covered with snow, or chipped, the potential buyer could slip and fall. (Not a great first impression!) Pressure clean mildew and take the time to address oil stains.

- A clean house (inside and out!) portrays a well-taken care of house and truly makes a big difference. Use the checklist below to give your home a staging-acceptable cleaning!

❑ Front yard cleaning: power wash
  ○ House
  ○ Front porch
  ○ Front door
  ○ Awnings
❑ All bedrooms clean and orderly
❑ Clean bathrooms meticulously
  ○ Fixtures
  ○ Sink
❑ Shower – *no mildew or mold on door, floor, or walls*
❑ Cabinets wiped downand knobs are new looking
❑ Exterminate insect problems
❑ Remove extra hangers in laundry room
❑ Clean skylights and ventilation hoods
❑ Appliances – *sparkling, put away smaller ones*
❑ Floors swept and mopped; nothing is "swept under rug!"
❑ Carpets steam cleaned – *don't forget the baseboards*
❑ Polish interior woodwork
❑ All windows clean inside and out (screens and sills too)
❑ Pet odors eliminated

- ❏ Fireplace – remove ashes
- ❏ Clean pool or pond with surrounding walkways if necessary
- ❏ Dust everything – *behind the lamps, picture frames, houseplants*
- ❏ Garage
  - ○ Power wash floor and doors
  - ○ Streamline and straighten contents
  - ○ Sweep walls and ceiling – *remove cobwebs*

Repairing

Now that everything is streamlined and scrubbed, it's time to get to those pesky repair jobs. With the clutter gone and the house clean, it may be surprising to see how many little things need repairing. A house cannot sell for top dollar if any detail, large or small, is in less than perfect shape. Ignoring even a small problem may prevent a sale when the competition is fierce. Something seemingly trivial like a leaky faucet, a cracked entryway tile, or peeling paint send a warning signal to buyers: work, work, work, which costs money, money, and money. And these warning signals trigger a fear that even larger problems lurk beneath the surface. How, for example, do you feel when your tray table on the airplane won't work properly? Everyone knows that if a plane, car, even a house receives poor or insufficient maintenance, serious problems can quickly arise.

Neglect and the need for lots of repairs position your house as a fixer-upper, significantly narrowing the profile and the number of potential buyers and the price they will pay. There are people who look for homes that are fixer-uppers, but remember, they are looking for a great deal, while staging focuses on getting top dollar. When a house is in need of repairs, buyers will feel justified in making low offers, as they are likely calculating an inflated repair cost in their offer. Few buyers want to spend their own time, money, and effort on something that should have been fixed in the first place. Never underestimate the importance of repairing absolutely everything no matter how small—even that cracked switch plate. Don't let the little "*fix* its" *break* the sale.

At this point, you might be thinking, *Well, if the buyer is worried about repair costs, what's it going to cost* me? Repair costs are entirely dependent on the condition of your house and its contents. In general, basic maintenance expenses are a low-cost/high-gain proposition. Buyers will not pay top dollar for a house with a leaky roof, malfunctioning furnace, or faulty plumbing. While these major repairs are necessary to put your house at the top of the price range, don't expect to recoup *all* the replacement costs. You may have to settle for a lower offer than if you did not contract for those repairs, but every house needs a roof, a furnace, and plumbing, and buyers will expect—but not necessarily pay for—them to be in good condition.

Carpeting can be an expensive replacement but might be well worth the investment if the existing carpeting is extremely worn, irreparably stained, or out of style. If there are wood floors underneath old carpet, throw out the coverings and refinish the floors. Most people like the look of wood floors. If not, install a neutral sisal, seagrass, or Berber style carpet. Make sure the floor and wall coverings complement one another. If you stick to neutral colors, they all show well together. New carpeting and freshly painted walls will set your house firmly at the top of the price range—possibly even pushing into a higher bracket.

All that said, don't let major repairs stand between you and the price you want. You can offer a repair allowance, but chances are if you go ahead and make repairs yourself, it will cost less than what you would have to reduce your price. Keep in mind that most buyers are looking for move-in condition, and having to make immediate, especially large, repairs will be seen as a negative, no matter who pays for them. A modest amount of money spent for small repairs may result in increased profits or a faster sale.

It likely goes without saying, but a word of caution: don't try to cover up problem areas. Homeowners are obligated by law to disclose any known defects, and most cities require an inspection certificate before a home can be put on the market. Buyers will often include an inspection as a contingency in the offer to purchase. They will hire professional home inspectors to analyze house features such as the roof, mechanical systems, interior and exterior condition, and any appliances that remain. Inspectors look for both existing and potential problems, so repairing flaws properly and immediately will save time and stress after you receive an offer. Consider investing in a seller's inspection, hiring a home-inspection company or engineer yourself to discover the problems ahead of time. They will conduct a thorough inspection and supply you a report that will inform you of problems you might not see. This way, you can deal with the issues *before* they appear on the buyer's inspection report. You might even be able to include the cost of an inspection in your selling price, and if you share the report with buyers, it will build confidence about the condition of your house. In addition, some home sellers purchase a home warranty plan, which guarantees a defect-free house for a specific period of time. In a competitive market, these protective and proactive strategies can set you apart.

Taking care of your home repairs also allows you to better compete with the new housing market, in which everything is working properly, updated, and brand-new. This can be a real advantage in a down market because the cost of a new home is drastically cut because the demand is low. According to FirstResearch.com for May 2009, "In a large market, the demand for new single-family homes can change by 50 percent in just two years; in smaller markets the change can be 100 percent." This is a result of the economy and population shifts. In a hot market, newer homes have higher price tags, and the older ones seem more affordable. But in a down market, the challenge is not only competing against older homes but also against new homes at drastically lower prices. If relevant, get your home in the right working condition to compete with the large inventory of new homes.

Improvement	Typical Cost	Increase in Sale Price	Average Return/Gain after costs	% Agents who recommend
Lighten & Brighten	$86-$110	$768-$935	769%	84%
Clean & Declutter	$305-$339	$2,093-$2,378	594%	91%
Fix Plumbing & Electrical	$338-381	$922-$1,208	196%	63%
Landscape & Trim	$432-$506	$1,594-$1,839	266%	72%
Staging	$212-$1,089	$2,275-2,841	169%	76%
Paint Interior Walls	$1,453-$1,588	$2,342-$2,600	63%	69%
Kitchen/Bath Upgrades	$1,546-$2,120	$3,823-$4,885	138%	83%
Repair Floorings	$1,531-$1,714	$2,267-$2,589	50%	62%
Paint Exterior	$2,188-$2,381	$2,907-$3,233	34%	57%
Replace Carpeting	$2,602-$2,765	$3,585-$3,900	39%	65%

* Typical home characteristics for U.S. agents responding: 3 bedroom, 2 bath, 1,892 sq. ft., sale price $201,798 (May 2000). Survey reproduced by Steve Stewart Seminars. www.steve-stewart.com

In summary, it is very important not to give the buyer any excuse to *not* buy your house. If she sees a broken tile, she might think it all needs replacing, and that will cost a lot of money. Show them you love your house and have taken good care of it. Buyers only know what they see, not the potential. Make it easy for them to buy your house. Use the helpful checklist below.

- ❑ Check all lights. Are they working properly? Replace all burned out lightbulbs.
- ❑ Look for dark hallways and corners and increase the wattage of bulbs in those areas.
- ❑ Repair and repaint cracks on all walls and ceilings. Keep caulking on hand so the house is always ready.
- ❑ Repair or replace broken light switches and switch plates.
- ❑ Fix or replace worn out vent covers.
- ❑ Address any broken blinds or other window treatments.
- ❑ Listen for and fix any wobbly ceiling fans.
- ❑ Make sure all windows operate freely. If the seal is broken on a double-pane window, replace it.
- ❑ Check the bathrooms for any loose tiles and make any needed repairs.
- ❑ Check all bathrooms to ensure everything is working properly.
- ❑ All the kitchen appliances need to be working properly.
- ❑ All the house plumbing needs to be working properly.
- ❑ All windows and doors need to be working properly. Make sure to keep up with recaulking around windows.

- ❑ Walk around the house; check for broken tiles or any roof issues.
- ❑ Make any siding, stucco, brick repairs if needed.
- ❑ The Laundry room need to be working properly.
- ❑ Walk through the entire home, inside and out, looking for any repairs.

Step Five: Redesign

Now that everything is orderly, minimized, clean, and in good working order, it's time to rearrange, or as they say in the staging profession, redesign. In other words, it's time to set the stage! Redesign is the act (and art!) of arranging furniture, creating focal points, and accessorizing to create natural traffic flow and visual interest for the prospective buyer.

In extreme cases, redesign might even call for breaking down or repurposing a room. For example, a house may have a "problem room," such as one with too many doors. Or maybe it's too small and difficult to define in terms of function. In these cases, look to recent trends. Setting up a massage room, craft area, or even gift wrapping room might be more appealing to a large population of buyers than a trophy room. There was one beautiful home that was equipped with a bird aviary in the middle of the house. Because birds do not appeal to everyone, it was suggested to stage this area as a piano parlor, sitting room, or butler's pantry. If your home has a "cat room," restage it as an office since that would be more of a desired room for someone looking at houses. Another tip would be to convert seemingly useless corners or nooks (maybe a wide space under a staircase) into wine storage areas. The trick is to appeal to the masses and demonstrate ideas for how to use the space.

Creating Traffic Flow

An important aspect that sets a staged home apart from other homes on the market is the flow of traffic patterns. People should be able to walk effortlessly through a home. The first rule: a traffic pattern—the path people would innately take through a home—should move *around* natural conversation areas, not *through* them. Except in the case of a "dead-end room" (a room with one single entrance and exit), most rooms have traffic leading through them. In most instances, you must cross the living room to get to the porch, or the only way to the bathroom is through the bedroom. You will want to facilitate the natural walk patterns using strategies such as furniture arrangement and focal points. Here's one example. When decorating, accent tables are often used to allow comfort for everyone in the seating area. However, in staging, it is often common to *remove* some of the accent tables! Using less furniture opens the flow of traffic, and buyers can envision their own items fitting in. (Remember, too, you want more space for wheelchair accessibility and big families coming through your house.)

Arranging Furnishings

When it comes to determining where furniture should be placed, your first consideration should be the support of traffic flow. Long pieces of furniture that block traffic paths should be removed. If at all possible, avoid having even the corner of a piece of furniture protruding out into the path.

When it comes to redesigning, remember that all the furniture does not need to stay. You can move pieces around or store them—remember to minimize! For example, you don't really need to pair end tables; using different shapes and sizes of tables can create interest. And you might only need one. This is just one difference between selling a home and living in it. You want buyers to focus on your house and not all of the furniture.

To begin arranging furnishings in the staging process, break down the whole room—completely empty it! The best ideas for the room itself come from a fresh start. Find a holding area and move all accessories and artwork to this area. Group like items together—pictures, figurines, collectables, etc. Then remove all but the largest pieces of furniture. Next, assess the entire room.

Many rooms will have more than one area of interest: choose the most important. One way to find an area of interest is to assess the height of the room and determine the highest point. Notice the ceiling: look for beams, cutouts, stenciling, or other points of interest. You will want to feature, not screen, these points of interest with the strategic positioning of furniture. Also, check to see if there are angles or other components to be considered before you place furniture. Are you restricted by electronic wiring or built-in or heavy pieces that must not be moved? Check the shape of the rooms. Is the room square, rectangular, or angular? Each unique shape will offer its own set of options to complement the room. For example, if you have a square room that has two walls with windows adjacent to each other and two walls without windows, it might be interesting to put a larger piece of furniture in the corner between the two walls with no windows instead of just against the wall. Every house is different and so is every room, so don't feel like there is one set of rules. Go with what feels right and works well to make the house inviting.

Now you are ready to choose and place furnishings to show off the home's best assets. If there is a large rug, place it first. An area rug does not necessarily need to be square with the furnishings, especially in the living room—turning it at an angle to the furniture can create contrast and interest. Place the largest pieces of furniture next. Position furniture around a natural focal point, such as a large window, a fireplace, or an entertainment center. Try to center pieces along walls or under the highest beam of the room. At that same time, try not to put a sofa up against the wall. There are some rooms where you have no choice, but if it is possible, a sofa usually looks better "floating" in the room with some walking room behind it.

Another tip relates to scale: large scale pieces should go against large walls and smaller pieces against smaller walls. For example, a small chest of drawers against a large wall will look awkward and lost.

Keeping in mind the number one goal is to promote traffic flow, use furniture to *guide* buyers gracefully through the house. For example, a sofa, or a long narrow table consisting of right angles to the wall, can effectively cut off access to an area and make traffic flow in the right direction. When the furniture placement is right, buyers easily and comfortably walk into each room. You will know what is right by the feeling you get when you enter the room.

Don't allow furniture to overbear or prevent a natural, welcoming flow of your home. When all the large pieces are placed, bring in the smaller ones and decide which ones are necessary and/or add to the look and flow you are creating. You will know you are on the right path if you can easily walk through the room and it still feels cozy.

Effective furniture arrangement can even "correct" the shape of a room. By grouping furniture in sections, you can break up an overly long room into multiple, separately themed areas. For example, a large room could be divided using furniture arranged in several seating areas. And you can use area rugs to define seating areas. But beware of crowding a room. A good rule of staging is to allow about two feet between cocktail tables and the sofa or chairs for easy access. For the couch-to-coffee table ratio, try sitting down and allowing enough room so that your knees just barely touch the table.

Furniture should create "peaks and valleys," providing visual interest as the eye travels around the room. To achieve this effect, make sure that the tallest piece of furniture follows the tallest ceiling line. Angled lines work best in square and rectangular rooms or in rooms with an existing angle. Try to use the correct shape of furniture too. Specifically, try to use a round table in a dining room if the ceiling tray is round. Similarly, if the ceiling cutout is a rectangle, use a rectangular table.

Also, if a sectional is large and long, try using a coffee table that is a rectangle-shaped because it will look better than if it were square. The furniture placement should complement the room, not overpower it. Try these tactics to create harmony and help the buyer see the whole house.

Sometimes the most obvious solutions are not necessarily the best. For example, you may have noticed that certain walls seem predestined for furniture placement. Experiment by trying something atypical, such as angling the bed in the bedroom rather than centering it on the "evident" wall. Do the same in the dining room—turn the table at a diagonal or place it at right angles to a wall instead of centering it under the chandelier. To break tradition and create interesting appeal, resist the urge to line furniture along the perimeter of your rooms, leaving wide-open spaces in the middle. Also, let your furniture extend into the room—"float" instead of being flush against the walls. It looks better and is often much more functional. There are many people who buy a couch, put it against a wall, and it stays there for twenty years. Here's your challenge: pull that couch out into the room, closer to the fireplace, for example, and make the room cozier. This is not always possible, but if it is, it does look better than against a wall.

Once a buyer makes the commitment to enter your house, research says she can spend up to an hour studying it. For that time, your house is the only product the buyer is focused on. Each room provides the perfect palate to make dozens of first impressions (every room, every nook, and every cranny), all directed at moving the buyer from looking at your house to evaluating whether it could be her new home. Make sure your furnishings work in your favor.

Following is a general list of redesign tips and techniques for arranging furniture.

- ❑ Match size of furniture with size of space.
- ❑ Place heavy, oversized furniture across the room from other large, heavy furniture for a well-balanced room.
- ❑ Keep heavy furniture away from doorways and entry sight lines.
- ❑ Bring furniture into the room rather than lining it up against the wall.
- ❑ Angle furniture in a small room to make it feel larger, but not in a corner.
- ❑ Place furnishings at an angle in an empty room to add variety and interest.
- ❑ Use area rugs to define specific areas. Don't "float" them in the middle of a room.
- ❑ Create sight lines in a room by arranging furniture to flow from low to high points.
- ❑ If ceiling detail is one shape, try using furniture under it the same.
- ❑ If there are no dividers, create many areas by using area rugs and clusters of furniture.
- ❑ Make sure there is not too much furniture, only the basics needed.
- ❑ Consider the size of furniture and what fits best with it.
- ❑ Try not to block any windows with furniture.

Creating a Focal Point

An effective staging technique used in redesign is creating a focal point—a "carrot" for the buyer's eye. In staging, focal points are created and used to draw attention to a part of the house you want the buyer to notice and to assist the traffic flow. Sometimes, built-in architectural elements such as columns, archways, mantels, and crown molding can serve as strong focal points. Other items to help emphasize the features include a beautiful painting, a vertical statue, or an arrangement of flowers. Try to create a focal point in every room. This will help the buyer notice these architectural elements we want to show off. Begin by looking for a natural centerpiece or axis. To where is the eye instinctively drawn?

Consider a fireplace or window with a view. Sometimes the diagonal corner to a room's entry, most often the right corner, is where the eye is drawn first. Place an important or visually inviting piece there. You can create a focal point with a piece of furniture, such as an armoire or console, or a mirror or large painting. Even a piece of sculpture or floral arrangement can work well—as long as it isn't too personal. Use an area rug to anchor a focal point and decorate the room to flow to the focal point.

You can showcase a nice stairway and really bring it to life by using the wall space in one artistic swoop of picture arranging. Arrange framed pictures in a way that "guides" the buyer up—again, encouraging the flow of traffic. Remember to keep the pictures, paintings, or decorative pieces at eye level: it feels more comfortable for people of standard height. Use the banister as a vertical guidepost. Try stacking a pair of prints in the landing area on the wall, but don't overpower the staircase.

Accessorizing

It's time to create some of the final staging touches using artwork, lighting, floral arrangements, patterns, and other accessories. Redesign involves the enhancement of a room by artfully placing accessories to attract. This part of staging can be very exciting as you shop the holding area you created when emptying rooms for hidden treasures. The goal is to transform the home into an enticing place.

Begin by combining existing treasures to create fresh arrangements. To save money and time, always try to leverage what you already have, and work to make it even better for showing. You can do this by following a few basic principles. Key design elements to pay attention to are proportion, balance, color, size, shape, and scale. Once accomplished, your room will not only be well arranged but will *feel* well arranged. And remember, it is as important to *feel* the essence of a home as it is to see it.

Proportion and Balance

Let's examine proportion and balance. Proportion is the relation of one part of an object to the whole. For example, if you want to highlight the pool or lakefront, you might use a smaller grouping of furniture to accentuate the view. Select and plan appropriate proportions to create a comfortable feeling of continuity. This is accomplished by keeping accessories somewhat similar to help the rooms flow together. The size of an object to another must also be considered. Try to use accessories that are the right size for that area. For example, if you have a large coffee table, you can use a few books, some candlesticks, and possibly a floral. But if it's a small table, stick to smaller accessories, such as a votive candle, one book, or a single flower in a small vase. Another accessory that is quite useful is mirrors. Mirrors can add depth to a small room and make it appear larger. They can also be used as accents on wall units, bathroom walls, etc.

A well-staged home is also well balanced. Balance comes in two forms: symmetrical (even balance) and asymmetrical (uneven balance). Balance, like a focal point, helps guide the eye and makes the buyer feel comfortable. Ways to achieve balance include using objects equal in size on each side of something. An example would be a front door with two trees on each side. Placing something large on one side of a room without placing it on the other, or in a lesser amount, will create asymmetrical balance. Bear in mind that symmetrical arrangements come across as more formal, and asymmetrical ones appear more casual.

Contrary to what might be expected, you do not have to have two items exactly alike to create balance. For example, if you have a formal living room with a sofa on one side and a coffee table in the middle, you can place two chairs opposite the sofa. Although they are not the same, they are equal in the amount of space they occupy. Another example would be to use a sofa on one side of a family room and just one accent chair on the other: this technique achieves less formal and asymmetrical balance.

Also, you can balance opposite walls within a space or room by placing a large mirror on one wall and a grouping of artwork on the other that appears to be equal in landscape to the mirror.

When it comes to achieving balance, a good design rule is to use only one dominating pattern within the room. Patterns are visual blueprints such as stripes, polka-dots, florals, plaids, animal prints, etc. If using a pattern, make sure it does not compete with the view or architectural elements you are trying to show off. Also, all patterns should coordinate. For example, it's okay to use an animal print with stripes as long as the color scheme is the same. You don't want to create a busy look by adding too many patterns or blending patterns that clash, such as mixing florals with animal prints and stripes. Different patterns of furniture can be mixed with items such as pillows and throws. But again, be careful not to use too many patterns—try to stick with two per room. For bedding and accessories, use vertical stripes in a large room and horizontal stripes in a smaller room. As in clothing fashion, stripes can add length or height, depending on the desired effect.

As a general rule when staging, symmetrical balance is recommended because it is comforting to the eye. We might not even realize it, but when a room looks symmetrical, it seems more balanced, and we feel more at ease. Not all rooms can be perfectly symmetrical, and those rooms can be calming to the sense as well. Work with the room and do the best you can with what you have.

Asymmetrical balance has its place too when it comes to accessorizing. For example, odd numbers of decorative accessories are more interesting than even numbers.

Apply this concept when using a floral display: use three or five stems for a basic arrangement (rather than four or six).

When working with accessories, group by color, shape, like material or theme to maintain the feeling of balance and order. Pay attention to the shape of objects to make an arrangement more soothing. For example, place round objects on a round table, square on square table, and oval on oval table. This way, interesting pieces will capture attention from all angles, and this technique is simply more aesthetically pleasing.

Lighting

Lighting is addressed in the curb appeal section in terms of first impressions and safety, but when it comes to adding those finishing touches, there are other lighting techniques to try. For example, many professionals recommend arranging lighting in triangles for thorough coverage. This can be achieved by having a lamp on one end table, a floor lamp next to a chair, and possibly a chandelier above the central part of the room. Try not to back a floor lamp into a corner whenever possible. Be creative and put a small lamp in a wall unit or on a console or sofa table. You can also use spotlights on the floor that can project upward to illuminate a tree, a statuary piece, or architectural element.

It is important to have every room well lit, warm, and welcoming. Whether you use overhead, accent, or floor lighting, keep in mind the purpose of the room. For example, an office could be well lit and a master bedroom lit enough to show it off but also look romantic. Lighting is also nice if over a painting or statue.

Artwork

Pieces of art that are all around the room help to grab buyers' attention. Art has always evoked emotion. The right artwork for the home can captivate the buyer and make her feel "at home." Use artwork that is scenic, figurative, and abstract. It should not be too bold, too personal, or too colorful. If a piece is reflective of a person, it should be nebulous or figurative. Most art that depicts nature works well. Also, use artwork to intensify a room or lead the eye around the room. Just like the masters in art bring your eye around a painting, try to take the buyers' eyes around your house. For example, to accentuate lofted ceilings, use a vertical element to take the eye upward. When hanging a large piece, make sure it is properly sized for the wall: large art works on large walls and smaller pieces on small walls. Small pictures can be grouped and used on bigger walls; however, make sure that they are evenly spaced apart.

Also, try resting a piece of artwork on a shelf instead of photos. When grouping artwork on a wall, it is best to choose a theme and then hang artwork relating to that theme together. For example, you might have a set of paintings done of flowers; you can group them together all on one wall. Artwork gives ambiance to all rooms, even theaters, gyms, and bathrooms. Nicely framed movie pictures work in home theaters.

Remember to regard balance and scale when accessorizing with artwork. For example, when using art above a sofa, either select a piece that is about the same width of the sofa or use two to three smaller ones grouped together to take up the same amount of space.

Again, art pieces should be proportional to the size of wall they are on. This is also true for vases, statues, and other art pieces. A piece of art on a pedestal can be perfect against a wall or in a niche. Another effective technique is to group odd numbers of items of different heights, such as a set of vases on a surface in a cluster. Also, try using risers to create different heights in a grouping of same size items.

Art can even facilitate traffic flow. For example, choose a tall piece of art or pieces of art that are all around the room to help grab buyers' attention. Just like with furniture, you can use pieces of art and even floral arrangements to create peaks and valleys as well as to create interest.

Many of the same rules apply as with lighting: don't, for instance, back a plant tightly into a corner. Instead, bring it out and offset it to one side just slightly. Try using an accent light from the floor or stringing clear lights on the plant to add soft accent lighting to your room. This is quite effective, especially around the holidays. Greenery also makes a room come alive and can create focal points. Small plants (healthy ones or artificial ones) look particularly nice on bookshelves, next to or on top of books. Trees and plants in the house can add balance and also make the room more welcoming. Other plant life that make a room warm and inviting are orchids and seasonal flowers. In addition to greens and flowers, branch and bush cuttings can be made into attractive arrangements.

Color

Of all the redesign elements, color elicits the greatest emotional response. Color can be used to give people a feeling of well-being, expand space, create certain moods, give or take away the illusion of light, or influence the way people will react. While sticking to neutrals is best for walls, flooring, and home exteriors, when it comes to accenting, color is the key. The right color can make a person feel at ease; likewise, the wrong color can make them feel agitated. Determining the right color for each area can be achieved by looking at the flooring material and major décor of the house. Try, for instance, to pull a neutral color from the flooring. For example, if the floor material is stone, choose one of the beige tones in the stone and go with that for your walls.

Color should be harmonious throughout the home. Harmony implies pleasing arrangements of parts, whether it is music, poetry, or even color. Creating home harmony in staging engages the viewer and creates an inner sense of order as well as balance in the visual experience. Without harmony, a visual experience can feel chaotic or even bland.

Warmer hues such as yellow, cream, beige, and some shades of taupe and green are excellent choices that evoke feelings of home and comfort. These work well in Mediterranean style homes and many others. However, if the home is ultra-contemporary and has a lot of concrete, go with cooler tones such as silver, blue, putty, gray, and green. When making color decisions, remember to play off the flooring shades. For example, if the tiles are in the blue/grey tones, you would not paint the walls yellow. Instead, a nice putty color would complement these tiles' tones. Conversely, if the floor tile is a beige travertine, many beige-yellow combinations would work and "feel" better than if the walls were painted gray. Never mix blue-based colors with yellow-based colors, as they will not look harmonious together.

Another approach is to use a color scheme based on nature. Why do we feel so at ease when looking at a sunset or a nature preserve? Nature provides a perfect departure point for color harmony. Also, you could try a monogamous color scheme. Monochromatics involves using one color (hue) predominately, which gives a harmonious feeling throughout the home. You can add accent by varying tints, tones, and shades within the same color scheme. Using tone on tone and staying within the same color but varying the intensities of the color can create a perfect composition. A monochromatic color scheme in light, cool tones will visually expand space. The paint companies have made it easy by showing colors in groupings. Use these tools as a guide for coordinating color for main rooms and accent rooms.

Another idea for accenting is to use a color scheme based on the use of white and one other color. You may use white as the dominant or the secondary color. Use the dominant color on the largest areas and the secondary color in the accessories and smaller pieces, or in different rooms. Add neutrals to finish off and give the whole home a harmonious look. When using contrasting colors, be proportionate. The general rule to follow is the brighter the color, the smaller the area in which it should be used. In other words, use a light or more neutral color on the large expanses in a room and confine bright or darker colors to accent areas. Of course, when staging a home, try to stay away from too bright colors. Consider this: just as a bright red stop sign is intended to stop a car, a red room will bring the flow and the eye to a halt!

Sometimes a darker shade will work in a room that receives direct sunlight. Color can be tricky, especially the way light plays into it. If you find a room looks too dark, try using more lighting or a different kind of lighting. Different bulb strengths or different shades or color of glass offer completely different looks. The goal is to light the room but not so brightly that it's not inviting.

When experimenting with colors, try painting a large patch of a few colors on a wall and look at it at different times of the day and with different lighting sources. You may be surprised how different a large wall looks after painting it because you had envisioned a different look from just using a small swatch. Be extra careful with the color red. While a red exterior front door shows nicely, avoid red interior walls when staging. The way light reflects on a wall can really vary, and different textures can change the way it looks too. Compensate for the effects of reflection by using a flat wall finish instead of semi-gloss or high gloss options.

Finally, you can also use color to create illusions to help with the principle of balance covered earlier in this chapter. For example, variance in color selections from light to dark can make a room appear larger or smaller. By selecting window treatments and wall colors that fade into the walls or surrounding elements, you can deemphasize unfavorable architectural features, like out-of-date pillars or niches. Alternatively, use a bright or contrasting color to call attention to assets and centers of interest. In other words, use color when you can to downplay the negatives and bring attention to the positives. Below is a summary of color principles and tips.

- Texture and light will change the color. If the colored wall will be facing a window that gets direct sunlight, it will seem much lighter. Also, texture will reflect light in a different way by reflecting light and looking lighter and darker on the same wall.

- The most successful way to combine colors together is to select the preferred dominant color and a group of related colors.

- Try contrasting colors with the preferred colors to see which contrasting color is the best.

- Rooms that are successfully decorated usually have the color scheme based on tones of one dominant color. Only one color should dominate. Use contrasting colors as accents in small amounts.

- Follow this basic rule: Only one color should be the dominant color; then introduce some contrast as accents in small amounts.

- Do not use too many colors. Several bold colors will seem to be fighting to dominate and make the room appear busier and smaller. Neutral colors make a room appear larger.

- Fewer colors and neutral colors make a room appear larger.

- Bolder colors jump out at you and can make a room smaller.

- Neutral colors are more subdued and make a room appear larger.

- A well put together color scheme can unify and blend un-unified furnishings or different styles and periods.

- Balance color throughout the room.

- On larger areas, keep the tone of the color less intense.

- Light colors reflect the sun much more effectively than darker colors. And remember, walls with direct sun will look much lighter during the day.

- White and black are neutral colors and can be used with most color combinations.

- In smaller rooms use less intense, lighter colors, and fewer patterns appear larger rather than smaller.

- Use the brightest intensity colors in the smallest areas. This tactic works best in accessorizing and accent pieces.

- Darker, deeper and warm colors will make a room appear smaller and more closed in.

- Sometimes deeper colors will work in an area that gets an abundance of natural light.

- Pastel and paler colors reflect light and expand space.

- Darker, warm colors have the tendency to close in a room.

- Large rooms can be made much more intimate with warm colors. Warm colors absorb light requiring more natural or artificial lighting. Use warm colors on high ceilings to lessen the expansive feeling of too much space. Also, use lighter colors on ceilings that are too low and feel claustrophobic.

Step Six:
Create Ambience

So far, you have created a sense of spaciousness, cleanliness, good repair, low maintenance, and intriguing visual appeal. Now for the *wow* effect! The last step in staging is what can really captivate the buyer—to incent them to remember your home over all others. It's time for the dramatic effects of creating ambience—the last step before opening the curtains.

Ambience is the secret weapon to creating a memorable feeling that lasts beyond the tour and makes the buyer want to come back to your house ... *to live.* Keep in mind that buyers are looking for a house that meets their physical *and* psychological needs and that most sales are emotionally based. This last step reaches the psychological needs of home buyers. It puts the finishing touches on selling a lifestyle, a new life, a new beginning.

The real secret to creating ambiance is staging rooms to generate feelings—every area and around every corner—that make buyers feel a visceral connection to your home. With methodical and imaginative staging, you create impressionable moments. Buyers want to feel comfortable and to enjoy a place of beauty and harmony, a haven from the hustle of daily living—a space to be proud to show family and friends. To succeed at selling your house quickly and profitably, you will want to evoke those very feelings.

Ambience appeals to all the senses, not only vision, but touch, smell, hearing, even taste. The more senses you reach with your staging messages, the more successful the communication.

Ambience is important in *all* areas of the home. The entryway, as mentioned earlier, needs to be inviting. The master bedroom should look restful and romantic. The dining room should be elegant or dramatic. Ambience throughout the house ensures that buyers are constantly surprised and delighted at what they find. A glass vase filled with elegant roses greets buyers in the entryway; luxurious towels and soaps in the bathroom make a visitor feel special; the good smells of baking in the kitchen lure people in (this can be real or simulated with potpourri, plug-ins, or candles), and a playfully arranged stuffed-animal tea party in a child's room will put a smile on anyone's face.

Think about playing a soft jazz or classical station, and turn the volume up loud enough to be heard throughout as much of the house as possible without being too loud for the room in which it originates. Soothing music can add dimension and warmth to rooms without the buyer even being aware that she is listening to music. There's a reason why department stores play music in the background—people linger longer and buy more. It's subtle, simple, and yet immensely helpful.

Having a home with ambience gives you the upper hand in any real estate market. Every space, inside and out, of your house is a communication opportunity. While the first five steps send buyers messages, ambience adds an even stronger message, suggesting easy living, family gatherings,

or an abundance of personal time. Staging a kitchen area, for example, with an open cookbook, simmering spices, and a beautiful display of vegetables invites buyers to imagine the good times and warm feelings that lay in store.

When your house is the one the buyers lose their hearts to, the competition does not stand a chance. Many ambiance techniques are neither difficult nor expensive. Try some of the subtle suggestions below, especially for open houses.

- Fresh flowers in the foyer

- A bowl of candy or popcorn in a movie room

- Marshmallows on sticks in an outdoor patio area

- A bucket of champagne with two glasses, fancy towels, tea candles, and luxurious soap next to the master bath

- A dining room set with the best of your serving pieces

- A tea set outside on an open terrace

- Patio furniture and topiaries in a patio area to make it look even more inviting

- A kitchen table set and a patio set with trees, candles, and greens to make it look dynamic

- A dining room with fresh, fragrant flowers and the look of spring

- A lit fireplace (or candles in the warmer months)

- Open drapes and blinds

- Cedar chips in closets and drawers

- Cookies in the oven

- Something fragrant simmering on the stove

- A tray on the master bed with a newspaper and plates and napkins

- Fancy chocolate on master bed when linens pulled back on nightstand or next to champagne set with tub

- Music playing throughout house

Notes

Notes

THE EMOTIONS OF STAGING

Sometimes the inevitable act of moving results in anxiety and apprehension for family members. Perhaps you have been in the community a long time, and you've established roots and friendships. Maybe your children were raised in this home. And maybe you really do not *want* to move, but a job transfer is inevitable. This makes the decluttering and packing experience even more stressful and staging really more valuable.

Staging is an objective process. It is a systematic way to get your home ready to sell. It might be easier to follow the recommended steps to get the end result instead of wondering what to do first. This book was designed to make it easy for you to navigate through the process of getting your home ready to sell for the most amount of money in the least amount of time.

If you have children, make a special effort to include them in all stages of the move. Since their world centers on home and friends, changing those factors can be difficult and scary for them. Ask for their suggestions and encourage them to share their ideas. Maybe start planning the décor in their new room in their new house. Involving kids in the process of staging gives them the opportunity to talk about their feelings, helping them adjust better to the move. Turn moving into an adventure and ease the transition to a new home. There are times when a member of a household who does not want to move actually sabotages the sale of a house. Teenagers, for example, often struggle the most with a move, and raging hormones might motivate negative actions to hinder the sale of their family's home just to stay near their friends. Getting your teenager on board early will ease your transition later on.

When your house is for sale, it is first and foremost a product, like thousands of products or sale every day in grocery stores, shopping malls, and catalogs. Manufacturers go to great lengths to position their products correctly in the mind of their target audiences. They use advertising, point-of-sale displays, pricing, and packaging to reach the consumer. Likewise, properly packaging your house will speed up the important shift in a buyer from seeing just a three-bedroom, two-bath house to seeing a home in which they begin to imagine living. The biggest hurdle you will have to cross as a seller is thinking of your house as a product to be sold and detaching from it emotionally. The sooner you treat your house like a product and not a home, the easier it will be for you to see what needs to be done to stage the house.

You need to separate the warm memories you have experienced in the house and the opportunity you have to sell your house. When you begin decluttering, take that time to reminisce about your family and moments and the joy you will have of putting everything out in a new home.

Depending on size and condition, if it is occupied or vacant, staging can be an hour consultation to a few weeks' production. Some homes just need some polish and can be done in a day or two, while others need to be repaired. The results will be spectacular whether you dress your house in a day or a month.

You might be wondering how you can live in a house that is positioned, packaged, and staged to sell. It will not feel natural, and it should not. A house packaged to sell has a completely different purpose than a house packaged for living. The good news is your home will not be on the market for long. We have been told by some homeowners that they need to live there and that the buyers will have to look over the dirty dishes, etc. The fact is that some people will walk out if they think the house is dirty, and if you want to sell it fast and for the most amount of money, then it's worth the extra effort. You have to prepare yourself to *work*, as there are no shortcuts, but the rewards of your work will be attaining the ultimate goal to sell your home.

Lastly, take it in baby steps. Preparing for a move can feel overwhelming—it seems like so much needs to be done. However, my hope is that if you follow the steps in this book and use the checklists, you will find the process less stressful and more rewarding in the long run—maybe even a little fun at times!

THE ART AND APPLICATION OF FENG SHUI

Feng Shui—pronounced "fung shway"—is a five-thousand-year-old Chinese concept focused on the arrangement of an environment and its elements to increase energy, or *Chi*. Chi, pronounced "chee," is the energy or life force that gives a home order. According to ancient beliefs and modern day translations, Chi brings happiness, prosperity, luck, and longevity. In more simplistic terms, Feng Shui is the art of placement, arrangement, and balance in harmony within the environment to bring prosperity.

Many professionals advise incorporating this concept into home staging for several reasons. The first reason relates to cleaning and organizing. Getting your home in proper Feng Shui will help you get organized and achieve the proper flow throughout the home. Feng Shui literally translates to "wind and water." The ancient Chinese believed that if we live in balance with the order of the world (Earth's winds and waters), we could attract fortune and prosperity. If this concept and its possibilities appeal to you, whenever possible, incorporate views of water, fountains, and birdbaths in your creation of focal points and traffic flow. The look and sound of water is pleasing and tranquil to nearly all potential buyers.

In Feng Shui, it is beneficial to create movement in your life. In staging, this translates to cleaning out and organizing closets, drawers, and storage areas by creating space. The theory is that by releasing what we no longer want or need, we create room for the next good thing to appear in our lives. Decluttering, a major step in staging, helps simplify our lives and increases the chance of a successful showing. *Could the next good thing be a potential buyer?* On a more pragmatic level, some of the primary principles that the Chinese use in cleaning, organizing, and accessorizing the home are to promote health, wealth, and happiness.

Also, it is said that Feng Shui will enhance clear thinking. By removing piles and excess "stuff" from horizontal surfaces, your desk, kitchen counters, etc., will look and function more efficiently. People lose focus if there are too many items in view or scattered about. Remember the old adage, "A messy desk is a messy mind." Apply basic principles of Feng Shui to achieve clear focus and an environment clear of clutter.

Feng Shui also increases prosperity. In staging, you can focus on abundance by hanging a picture of something that inspires you, such as a mountain or ocean scene, or a rendering of a place you want to go to. As discussed in step four of how to stage, the office is the recommended place to include personal items. So if the item that inspires you is personal, choose a nice frame or spot for it here.

Expanding your vision is yet another Feng Shui principle that works well with staging. By cleaning windows and mirrors, you open up a clear view of the world you live in. On a higher plane, expanding your vision allows more room for reflection, meditation, and focus on your dreams. *And* it looks clean and makes the house appear well maintained as well!

In essence, Feng Shui and staging work hand in hand. By cleaning and organizing your home, you are also creating movement in your life and getting ready to sell your home.

GOING GREEN:
THE ECO-SAVVY EDGE
FOR SELLING A HOME

There is no doubt the green campaign is here to stay, and just like in almost all other industries, there is a growing demand and commitment on the part of new home construction and real estate industries to do their part. This environmental concern has been around for years, but the next generation is even more informed and committed to protecting the environment. According to First Research for April 2009, today's teenagers, estimated at 31 million, represent one of the nation's fastest growing consumer segments. Although most teens aren't ready to buy homes today, the requirements they will want in a home should be in our minds when building and improving homes. They are eco-conscientious and passionate about saving the planet.

The U.S. baby boomers, the population born between 1946 and 1964, are already starting to retire. And the following generation, known as "Gen X," born between 1967 and 1979, which is about half the size of the Boomer population, is the next generation of home buyers. This generation is environmentally savvy, and many are willing to pay a premium for an environmentally and energy-efficient home.

Although a "green" home can cost 5 percent more than a conventional house, some lenders offer mortgage incentives for energy-efficient homes. Some of the green building innovations include more porous materials in walkways and patios to prevent erosion from rain run-off, engineered recycled lumber, and the conversion of wood or drywall construction waste outside into landscape mulch. In December 2007, the U.S. Green Building Council launched LEED for Homes, a green home rating system for assuring that homes are designed and built to be energy and resource efficient as well as healthy for occupants. Over seven hundred builders across the U.S. are participating in the LEED for Homes program (First Research Report, April 2009). In addition, builders are being asked to use more energy-savvy features, such as better insulation and tighter-fitting windows.

According to an article in the *Wall Street Journal*, a major shift for consumers is a higher interest in saving money on their energy costs over time. One builder, Kevin Enyert, in Lee Springs, Missouri, says he has picked up two contracts and possibly a third over the past six months from buyers who specifically requested energy saving features. According to Anjali Atharally in another article in the *Wall Street Journal*, people are willing to pay $1,299 for a washer that will save them ninety dollars a year.

Responding to this trend, at the International Builders show in January 2009, many companies showcased their new energy-efficient models. General Electric Company, for example, featured a hybrid electric water heater designed to save consumers about two hundred fifty dollars annually. Whirlpool Corporation claimed its Cabrio HE washer can save up to nine hundred dollars in lifetime water and energy costs, or ninety dollars a year. Kohler Company also introduced new toilets and faucets that save a family of four from ninety to two hundred dollars a year. There are several other companies going in this direction. According to Mark Delaney, director of the home industry sector at NPD Group, a market research firm, "If people can see in black and white that there is a cost savings involved, they are more inclined to buy it."

Some builders are also retrofitting existing homes to use energy better. For example, some builders are using an infrared camera to detect leaks in a house. Sealing the home could reduce energy usage by a significant amount.

In the last five years, there have been many articles reflecting homebuyers going green to cut bills. In this economy, consumers are increasingly more frugal and are looking for ways to save even after they purchase a home. There are many ways to improve your home and give it yet another edge over the competition—and one of those ways is by being eco-friendly. If you are remodeling, check with www.energystar.gov to see what appliances meet the federal government's Energy Star efficiency standards. You can also hire a professional to audit the energy use in your home. After doing so, you can make the improvements and share with the potential buyers your findings and what you did to remedy the inefficiencies. This is a wonderful sales feature.

If your home already has some of these features or you can easily obtain them, it would be another way to stand apart in your staging and selling process. For example, if your wood floors are made from recycled wood or any other improvements on air quality have been made, call those out to prospective buyers. Make sure this information is on the MLS and on any marketing material that is made. This is another advantage in a down market.

There are other ways you can do your part, such as recycling and using eco-friendly cleaning products. Recycling bins full of paper or plastic in your garage tell buyers you care about the environment the way you care about your home. Think about adding compost in an obscure place in your backyard. "Going green" is an advantage in up or down markets, so explore ways you can take advantage of this edge on selling your home—and for doing your part in improving the world we live in. Below are some additional green tips in regard to staging.

- Use water-based (latex) paint and primers whenever possible because they are lower in VOCs (volatile organic compounds) over oil-based paint. These chemical compounds that are found in many building products, including paint, adhesives, and colorants, can vaporize into the atmosphere, affecting indoor and outdoor air quality.

- Check with www.energystar.gov to see whether your appliances meet the federal government's Energy Star efficiency standards. Some of the older appliances might not only look outdated but be energy wasting as well. If you are thinking about making improvements, this is a good place to start and something else to point out to your realtor after your home is on the market.

- If you are building a spec home or doing some remodeling, consider adding a hookup in the garage for electric cars. This will certainly make your home look updated.

- If you are recarpeting, select a low-emission product and be sure to point that out.

- Natural ink removers: cover the stains with a little milk or rub with the cut side of half of a tomato. Rinse both treatments out well.

- For washing windows: You can make your own cleaner out of vinegar and water in a plant spray bottle. Vinegar cuts grease and brings out a good shine. You can also use old newspapers crumbled up to wipe off the vinegar-water solution. It works well, and you are thinking green.

- For cleaning carpet: To freshen your carpet inexpensively and ecologically, liberally sprinkle baking soda all over it. Leave for at least 20 minutes then vacuum thoroughly. Not only will your carpet be clean, you will have discouraged pests and neutralized odors.

- Removing discolorations on metals: For aluminum, boil natural acid by using onions, lemon juice, rhubarb or apple peels. Then let it cool and rub on discolored areas to brighten. For copper, rub with the cut side of a lemon dipped in salt to remove tarnish. You can also try filling a spray bottle with vinegar and three tablespoons of salt, and spray onto the copper. Let sit and rub clean.

BIBLIOGRAPHY

Barnett, Fiona and Roger Egerickx. *The New Flower Arranger: Contemporary Approaches to Floral Design*. London: Anness Publishing, 1995.

Beattie, Antonia. *Using Fung Shui: Easy Ways to Use the Ancient Chinese Art of Placement for Happiness and Prosperity*. Australia: Lansdowne Publishing, 2003.

Berges, Steve. *101 Cost Effective Ways to Increase the Value of Your Home: Featuring Projects That Will Add $1000 for $100,000 to the Value of Your Property*. Chicago: Pearborn Trade Publishing, 2004.

Burrell, Paul. *In the Royal Manner: Expert Advice on Etiquette and Entertaining from the Former Butler to Diana, Princess of Wales*. New York: Warner Books, 1999.

Effros, Bill. *How to Sell Your Home in 5 Days.* New York: Workman Publishing, 1993.

Englebert, Clear. *Bedroom Fung Shui.* Freedom, California: The Crossing Press, 2001.

House Beautiful editors. *House Beautiful Colors for Your Home.* New York: Hearst Books, 2008. www.sterlingpublishing.com

Hueston, Fredrick. *Marble and Tile: The Selection and Care of Stone and Tile Surfaces.* Orlando, Florida: NTC Publishing Company, 1996.

Irwin, Robert. *Home Sellers Checklist: Everything You Need to Maximize Profit, Save Time, and Keep Your Sanity!* New York: McGraw-Hill, 2004.

Kent, Cassandra, and Christine France, Julian Cassell, Peter Parham, and Pippa Greenwood. *10,001 Hints & Tips for the Home.* New York: DK Publishing Inc., 1998.

Kramer, Brian. *Trading Spaces: Color!.* TLC, 2003.

Kramer, Brian. *Trading Spaces $100 to $1000 Makeovers: Maximizing Your Decorating Dollars.* TLC, 2003.

Pennington, Ty. *Ty's Tricks: Home Repair Secrets Plus Cheap and Easy Projects to Transform any Room.* New York: Hyperion Books, 2003.

Tincher-Durik, Amy. *HGTV Before & After Decorating.* TLC, 2003.

Tincher-Durik, Amy, editor. *Trading Spaces: Ultimate Episode Guide.* TLC, 2003.

Walton, Stewart and Sally. *Instant Home Makeovers: High Impact Ideas to Transform Your Home.* New York: Anness Publishing, 2001.

Webb, Martha and Sarah Parsons Zackheim. *Dress Your House for Success: 5 Fast, Easy Steps to Selling Your House, Apartment or Condo for the Highest Possible Price!* New York: Three Rivers Press, 1997.

ABOUT THE AUTHOR

Megan Morris was raised in northern California and spent many summers working with her mother, an interior designer in San Francisco. After graduating from the University of Southern California with a Bachelor of Science degree, she worked in marketing and merchandizing as an art docent, investor, and business owner. Megan lived for several years in the Midwest and currently resides in Florida.

Megan is the founder of MHM Professional Staging Inc., a successful Home Staging, Decor and Events Company in Orlando, and has worked in home staging and design for the past ten years. Her expertise in visual displays and space planning has been recognized and honored in several design competitions and she has been hired as the lead set decorator for several commercials, including Nike, Werthers, New York Life,

VH1, and ESPN. Her background also includes marketing and merchandising when she worked for several department store chains inluding Nordstrom, Macy's, and Polo.

Megan has experienced the ups and downs of the real estate market firsthand. Through the rise and fall of home prices in California, Megan realized that the most successful sales all had one thing in common—the houses were staged. After moving to Florida and witnessing the upswing of the rapidly expanding market, it was evident yet again that the staged homes were the ones getting top dollar. Years later, as that market changed, again it was the staged homes that moved while the others sat idle. The process of evaluating, and later staging, homes, led Megan to develop a system that specializes in staging secrets. This book was written to give anyone the closely guarded tools of staging, enabling a seller the ability to sell any house in any market.

Megan has also co-authored two other books called *Trendsetters* and *Sold*.

Megan has given seminars to several different organizations regarding staging and is regarded as an expert in her field. Several articles have been written about her success in real estate magazines, and Megan's home was featured in *Frontgate Magazine*. Megan has also appeared on radio and television, including shows on Fox news, CNN, MSNBC, Bravo, The Food Network, and CNBC.

*You can contact Megan online
at the following sites:*

www.professionalstaging.com
twitter.com/mhmstaging
mhmprostaging.blogspot.com
facebook.com/celebritystyleestatevenues

Or you can reach Megan by mail:

6450 Kingspointe Pkwy. #4
Orlando, FL 32819

You can also reach Megan at

mhmprostaging@gmail.com

Notes

Notes

Notes